Cambridg

MW00584251

Elements in the

edited by
Yujin Nagasawa
University of Birmingham

THE DESIGN ARGUMENT

Elliott Sober
University of Wisconsin-Madison

CAMBRIDGE
UNIVERSITY PRESS

CAMBRIDGE
UNIVERSITY PRESS

University Printing House, Cambridge CB2 8BS, United Kingdom

One Liberty Plaza, 20th Floor, New York, NY 10006, USA

477 Williamstown Road, Port Melbourne, VIC 3207, Australia

314–321, 3rd Floor, Plot 3, Splendor Forum, Jasola District Centre,
New Delhi – 110025, India

79 Anson Road, #06–04/06, Singapore 079906

Cambridge University Press is part of the University of Cambridge.

It furthers the University's mission by disseminating knowledge in the pursuit of
education, learning, and research at the highest international levels of excellence.

www.cambridge.org
Information on this title: www.cambridge.org/9781108457422
DOI: 10.1017/9781108558068

© Elliott Sober 2019

First published 2019

A catalogue record for this publication is available from the British Library.

ISBN 978-1-108-45742-2 Paperback
ISSN 2399-5165 (online)
ISSN 2515-9763 (print)

The Design Argument

DOI: 10.1017/9781108558068
First published online: December 2018

Elliott Sober
University of Wisconsin-Madison

Abstract: This Element analyzes the various forms that design arguments for the existence of God can take, but its main focus is on two such arguments. The first concerns the complex adaptive features that organisms have. Creationists who advance this argument contend that evolution by natural selection can't be the right explanation. The second design argument – the argument from fine-tuning – begins with the fact that life could not exist in our universe if the constants found in the laws of physics had values that differed more than a little from their actual values. Since probability is the main analytical tool used, this Element provides a primer on probability theory.

Keywords: design, evolution, fine-tuning, probability

ISBNs: 9781108457422 (PB), 9781108558068 (OC)
ISSNs: 2399–5165 (online), 2515–9763 (print)

Contents

1 Introduction

Design arguments for the existence of God begin with observations, but so do other arguments for that conclusion. What is distinctive about design arguments is that they find goal-directedness in nature; the observed facts are said to obtain because God *wanted* them to.

Design argument fall in two broad categories, corresponding to two types of observation. *Cosmic* design arguments begin with an observation about the whole universe; *local* design arguments start with an observation about planet Earth.

The most famous design argument is local. We observe that the organisms around us are well adapted to their environments, and that the features that allow organisms to survive and reproduce are often complex and delicate. By delicate I mean that an adaptive structure would be unable to perform its function if any of its parts were removed or modified. The human eye has been cited for centuries as an example. I call local arguments about the adaptedness of organisms *biological design arguments*.

A much-discussed cosmic design argument is of more recent vintage. The laws of physics contain constants whose values can be ascertained by observations. The laws are said to entail that life would be impossible if those constants had values that differed more than a little from their actual values. The conclusion is then drawn that God exists and set the values of the physical constants so that life would be possible, that being one of God's goals. This is the *fine-tuning argument* for the existence of God.

There are cosmic design arguments that do not appeal to fine-tuning; some start with the premise that the universe is governed by simple laws (Swinburne 1968). And there are local arguments that seek to explain facts that are non-biological. For example, William Whewell (1833) argued that God arranged the Earth's daily cycle of dark and light to fit the human need for rest and work, and William Buckland (1836) contended that God put coal and iron in the ground for human benefit. Their books were two of the *Bridgewater Treatises*, a series devoted to exploring the "Power, Wisdom, and Goodness of God, as manifested in the Creation" (Robson 1990).

Although design arguments start with observations and end with the conclusion that God exists, there is often an intermediate step. First the argument moves from observations to the conclusion that an intelligent designer did the deed. Then comes the inference that that intelligent designer is God. This two-step format means that a design argument can succeed in its first step but flounder in its second. For example, even if the life forms we observe were the result of intelligent design, the possibility remains that the designer in question isn't God. Perhaps creating life from nonliving materials is something that a designer with merely human intelligence is capable of achieving. Until recently, this would have been an astonishing speculation; now the achievement seems to be just a matter of time.

Design arguments for the existence of God need to deploy some conception of what kind of being God is. I assume in what follows that if God exists, that being, by definition, intentionally created the universe. I say "intentionally" to distinguish God from a mindless Big Bang. By "universe" I mean the totality of objects, events, and processes that have spatiotemporal locations; "universe" is another name for nature. If God and nature are distinct, then God is *super-natural* (existing outside of space and time), not a part of nature at all. This means that none of the gods and goddesses of ancient Greece, who lived on Mount Olympus, was a God. Plato took that consequence in stride; he thought that immortal gods and goddesses, and mortal organisms as well, were created by a divine craftsman. Aristotle's God, however, is left out in the cold by my definition, and so is Spinoza's. Aristotle thought that the universe had no beginning; it has always existed and so it had no creator. For Aristotle, God is a pure contemplator, not a maker of things.[1] Similarly, Spinoza's God (whom he said is identical with nature) isn't a God, since his God does nothing intentionally. My working definition of "God" can be adjusted if need be; it is just a useful point of departure.[2]

Design arguments are part of *natural* theology, not *revealed* theology. They appeal to observations and theories that should be defensible without any prior religious commitment. They do not appeal to the authority of sacred texts or traditions. Design arguments are intended to obey the same rules that govern scientific arguments. The justifications they offer for thinking that God exists are supposed to be similar to the justifications that science provides for thinking that genes and electrons exist. Design arguments are miles away from the idea that religious convictions should be based on faith rather than evidence.

Different design arguments are often formulated with different competing hypotheses in mind. For example, when the biological design argument asserts that organisms have complex adaptations because God made them so, the alternative hypothesis now considered is usually the Darwinian theory of evolution by natural selection. However, when the fine-tuning argument asserts that the physical constants have their values because they were set by God, the alternative

---

[1] Sedley (2007) discusses the design argument in ancient Western philosophy.

[2] In Hume's 1779 *Dialogues Concerning Natural Religion*, the three protagonists define God as the cause of the universe, and they agree at the outset that God exists. My definition differs from Hume's, but, like Hume's, it leaves open whether God is omnipotent, omniscient, and perfectly benevolent.

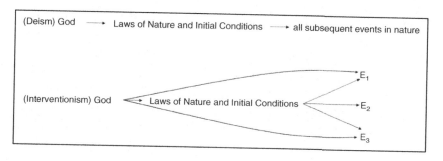

Figure 1 Deism and interventionism

hypothesis considered isn't evolutionary theory; rather, it's the hypothesis that the values of the physical constants were set by a mindless random process. Each design hypothesis competes with an alternative hypothesis that postulates a mindless process, but the two mindless processes are only superficially similar. The chance hypothesis considered in the fine-tuning argument does not invoke natural selection, mutation, or common ancestry. In addition, it's misleading to say that the results of natural selection are matters of chance (a point I discuss in Section 3).

The fine-tuning argument and the biological design argument are broadly similar. Both assume that God is well disposed to the existence of living things. The former says that God created the laws governing the universe so that organisms would be *possible*; the latter says that God contrived to make them *actual*. Yet, there are important differences between the two arguments. As noted, they consider different competing hypotheses. In addition, there are objections that apply to one of them that do not pertain to the other, or so I argue in what follows.

Another reason to separate biological design arguments from the fine-tuning argument can be seen by considering the two views of how God is related to nature that are depicted in Figure 1. The first is *deism*; it says that God creates the universe (thereby setting its initial conditions) and creates the laws of nature, and that all subsequent natural events are due to the initial conditions and the laws; God never intervenes in nature after the ball starts rolling.[3] The second view says that God creates the universe and the laws, but then sometimes intervenes in nature to influence what subsequently happens. I call this *interventionism*.[4] Interventionists don't need to assert that *everything* that happens in nature requires God's special attention. In Figure 1, event E_2

---

[3] The term *deism* is sometimes used to denote a rejection of revealed religion. That is not how I use the term.

[4] Theologians often use the term *intervention* to mean that God violates laws of nature. That is not how I use the term.

happens just because of the laws and initial conditions without God needing to reach in and tinker. E_1 and E_3 are different; true, the laws and the initial conditions *help* make them happen, but God lends a hand as well.

The fine-tuning argument is perfectly compatible with deism, but biological design arguments usually are not. This is because biological design arguments are usually formulated by creationists who argue that God reached into nature and created organisms. Creationists think that natural selection is incapable of producing the complex adaptive features we observe; indeed, they think that no mindless process is capable of delivering that result. Creationists reject *theistic evolutionism*, the view that Darwinian evolution is the sufficient mechanism that God chose to use so that organisms would come to have their adaptive features. Theistic evolutionism is compatible with deism, but creationism is interventionist.[5]

People who now call themselves "intelligent design theorists" do not like being called "creationists," but I sometimes do so in this Element. They bristle at that label because there are two differences between the two theories. Creationism rejects the thesis that all present life on Earth traces back to a single common ancestor, whereas intelligent design theory (Behe 1996; Dembski 1998a; Meyer 2009) is formulated so as to be neutral on that question. The second difference is that creationism asserts that God is the designer who built organisms, whereas intelligent design theory does not say who the designer is. ID theory is thus logically weaker than creationism in the technical sense that creationism entails ID, but not conversely. Although the two *theories* are different, the two groups of *theorists* are mostly on the same page. ID theorists usually reject universal common ancestry, and they usually think that God is the builder of organisms; they just don't want to put those propositions into their official theory.[6] Even though ID theory doesn't use the G-word, and this Element is about design arguments for the existence of God, the arguments made by ID theorists are relevant to the task at hand.

Deism and interventionism agree that if you look at any event in nature and trace back its causes, you will sooner or later reach the hand of God. There is no difference in this respect between the human eye and a stone found on a heath. However, this similarity between eye and stone is compatible with there being an *evidential* difference. Friends of the design argument often hold that some observations give you evidence for the existence of God while others do not.

---

[5] It is well known that Darwin opposed creationism; it is less widely recognized that he was a deist when he wrote *Origin of Species* (Sober 2011).

[6] For discussion of their motivation for not putting the word "God" into ID theory, see Forest and Gross (2004); for an argument that ID theory is committed to the existence of a supernatural designer, see Sober (2007b).

William Paley takes this line in his 1802 book *Natural Theology*, as do the predecessors from whom he drew and the successors who gave him undeserved credit for an argument he did not invent.[7] For them, the eye tells you something that the stone does not.[8] Friends of the fine-tuning argument are entitled to take the same stand, holding that facts about physical constants provide evidence of God's plan even though other physical facts do not.

Design arguments differ from one another by beginning with different premises, but they also sometimes differ over what they take their premises to show. Four possible conclusions might be drawn from premises that include observations:

(1) The observations prove that God exists.
(2) The observations show that God probably exists.
(3) The observations are evidence that God exists.
(4) The observations favor the hypothesis that God exists over a given alternative hypothesis.

Although (2) uses the word "probably" while (3) and (4) do not, I think the evidence mentioned in (3) and the favoring mentioned in (4) need to be understood probabilistically. This is why I provide a primer on probability in the next section. That primer helps clarify how (2), (3), and (4) are distinct. But before we get to all that, let's consider possibility (1).

Can the existence of an intelligent designer be deduced from the characteristics you observe an object to have? It can, if you add a premise:

Object *o* has characteristic *C*.
All objects with characteristic *C* are intentionally caused to have that trait by an intelligent designer.

An intelligent designer intentionally caused *o* to have *C*.

Notice that this form of argument is deductively valid, meaning that if the premises are true, the conclusion must be true.

What characteristics can plausibly be inserted into this argument form? If we let *C* be the characteristic of being well designed, and we assume that the slogan "no design without a designer" is true by definition, then the second premise is

---

[7] Jantzen (2014) argues that Paley copied word for word from Bernard Nieuwentyt in presenting the watch argument. Branch (2017) discusses this and other sources of Paley's.

[8] Shapiro (2009) contends that Paley intended his design argument to be compatible with deism, in that it allows there to be a proximate natural mechanism that God introduced so that adaptive contrivances would arise.

true. However, this choice makes trouble for the first premise. To avoid begging the question, design arguments need to discuss a characteristic that you can see attaches to an object without your needing to already have an opinion as to whether the object was intelligently designed. Biologists now use the term "well designed" with a more neutral meaning – that organisms have features that permit them to survive and reproduce. Biologists often take design in this sense to be evidence for the mindless process of natural selection and reject the slogan just mentioned. Biologists and other scientists often feel the same way about a similar slogan, that "there can be no laws without a law giver." They now generally think they can discuss the laws of nature without committing to the existence of an agent who put those laws into effect.

Thomas Aquinas's fifth proof of God's existence, presented in his thirteenth-century *Summa Theologica*, is deductive. He says that entities that "act for an end" and that do not have minds must have been caused to act that way by an intelligent being. For Aquinas, objects act for an end when their behavior is goal directed. Mindless plants and animals are obvious examples.[9]

Atheists, agnostics, and theists can agree that mindless organisms produce goal-directed behavior (as when sunflowers turn toward the sun), so this premise in Aquinas's argument is not in doubt. Trouble arises with the second premise. How can you tell that intelligent design is the only possible cause of what you observe? Aquinas thought that *all* mindless objects that produce goal-directed behavior must be caused to act that way by an intelligent designer, but Darwin's (1859) theory of natural selection shows that a mindless process is quite capable of yielding that result. Present-day creationists concede this point; they retreat from Aquinas's bold claim to something more modest, insisting that there is a special subclass of adaptive features that natural selection cannot produce. Sometimes they grant that mindless natural selection can produce microevolution (which includes adaptive improvements that evolve in a single enduring species), but insist that macroevolutionary novelties (the emergence of new "kinds" of organism) are beyond selection's reach (Numbers 2004). At other times, they argue that natural selection cannot produce adaptations that are "irreducibly complex" (meaning complex structures that would be unable to perform their function if any part were removed), but allow that natural selection can produce adaptations that aren't irreducibly

---

[9] As stated, Aquinas's argument commits a logical fallacy. The premise that each mindless object that acts for an end was created by some intelligent designer or other does not entail that there is a single designer who created all the mindless objects that act for an end. Reasoning in this way is like thinking that "everybody has a birthday" entails that there is a single day on which everybody was born. That's why I call this error *the birthday fallacy* (Sober 1990). Adding a premise can, of course, make Aquinas's argument deductively valid, and it has been argued that Aquinas had some such additional premise in mind.

complex (Behe 1996). Even if creationists were right in what they say about natural selection, that would not be enough to make the deductive argument work. The second premise in the argument displayed earlier doesn't just say that the mindless processes we now know about never produce objects that have characteristic *C*; it also says that the same is true of all the mindless processes we don't know about. Establishing that thesis is a tall order.

After describing some probability tools in the next section, I put those tools to work in Section 3 by further analyzing how design arguments differ. In Section 4, I discuss the biological design argument and the criticisms that creationists have made of evolutionary theory. In Section 5, I examine the fine-tuning argument. I don't spend much time describing the details of biological adaptations or of physical laws. This is a brief volume of philosophy, not science journalism, so broader issues about reasoning will always be at center stage.

2 A Probability Primer

Design arguments are often formulated by using the concept of probability, and even when they are not, probability is a useful tool for analyzing them. Here are the basics.

2.1 Axioms

You are about to be dealt a card from a deck. Consider the proposition that the card will be an ace of spades. Assigning a probability to that proposition requires assumptions. For example, if you assume that the deck of cards is standard and that the dealer is dealing you cards "at random," you can conclude that the probability is $\frac{1}{52}$. Change those assumptions and this probability assignment may be incorrect. To make the role of assumptions explicit, I sometimes represent the probability of proposition *H* by writing $\text{Pr}_A(H)$, rather than $\text{Pr}(H)$, to indicate that the probability assignment is based on the assumption that *A* is true.

Three axioms define the mathematics of probability; they are adapted from Kolmogorov (1950):

(Axiom 1) $0 \leq \text{Pr}_A(H) \leq 1$.
(Axiom 2) $\text{Pr}_A(H) = 1$ if *A* deductively entails *H*.
(Axiom 3) $\text{Pr}_A(H \text{ or } J) = \text{Pr}_A(H) + \text{Pr}_A(J)$ if *A* deductively entails that *H* and *J* are incompatible.

Each holds for any assumptions *A* you please. Axiom 1 indicates that probability can be understood as a mathematical function that maps propositions onto numbers between 0 and 1, inclusive. Here are three consequences of the axioms:

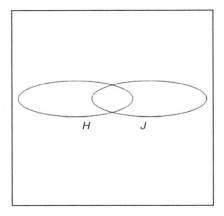

Figure 2 A Venn diagram of propositions *H* and *J*

- Tautologies have a probability of 1 and contradictions have a probability of 0.
- If propositions *H* and *J* are logically equivalent, then $Pr_A(H) = Pr_A(J)$.
- **The theorem of total probability:** $Pr_A(H) = Pr_A(H\&J) + Pr_A(H\&notJ)$.

The third consequence follows from the second and Axiom 3.

Axiom 3 describes how the probability of a disjunction is settled by the probabilities of its disjuncts if the disjuncts are incompatible. What happens if the disjuncts are compatible? You can visualize the answer by using a Venn diagram (named after John Venn, 1834–1923). Figure 2 shows a square in which each side has a length of one unit. Each point in the square represents a possible way the world might be. A proposition can be associated with a set of points in the square – the set of possible situations in which the proposition is true. The area of the square is 1, which conveniently is also the maximum value that a probability can have. Tautologies are true in all possible situations; they fill the whole unit square. The figure represents propositions *H* and *J* as two ovals. Their intersection – their area of overlap – represents the conjunction *H&J*. Since there is overlap, the two propositions are compatible; there are possible situations in which both are true. I hope the Venn diagram makes it obvious that

$$Pr(H \text{ or } J) = Pr(H) + Pr(J) - Pr(H\&J).$$

The reason for subtracting Pr(H&J) is to ensure that the area of overlap is not double-counted. When Pr(H&J) = 0, this equality reduces to the special case described in Axiom 3.

What about the probability of conjunctions? This is where the concept of **probabilistic independence** gets defined:

Propositions H and J are probabilistically independent, according to assumptions A, precisely when $\Pr_A(H\&J) = \Pr_A(H) \times \Pr_A(J)$.

If you flip a fair coin twice, the probability of getting a head on the first toss is $\frac{1}{2}$ and the probability of getting a head on the second is also $\frac{1}{2}$. The tosses are probabilistically independent, so the probability of getting heads on both tosses is $\frac{1}{4}$. The outcome of the first toss doesn't change the probability you assign to the second. That's the real world, but things might have been otherwise. Suppose you lived in a world in which there are two kinds of coin: 50% have two heads and 50% have two tails. You select a coin at random and toss it repeatedly. Under the assumptions stated, $\Pr_A$(heads on the first toss) = $\Pr_A$ (heads on the second toss) = $\frac{1}{2}$. However, it's also true that $\Pr_A$(heads on both the first and the second toss) = $\frac{1}{2}$. Independence fails. In this fanciful world, knowing the outcome on the first toss gives you information about the second.

Probabilistic independence and logical independence are different. Propositions X and Y are logically independent precisely when all four conjunctions of the form $\pm X \& \pm Y$ are logically possible (i.e., noncontradictory). For example, "it is raining" and "you are carrying an umbrella" are logically independent of each other. However, if you follow the advice of reliable weather forecasters, these propositions will be probabilistically dependent.

2.2 The Probability That an Improbable Event Will Happen Eventually

Assuming that the deck of cards before you is standard and that you're going to draw a card at random, the probability of your getting the ace of spades is $\frac{1}{52}$. What is the probability of getting the ace of spades at least once if you draw 100 times from the deck, each time returning the card you drew to the deck and then reshuffling? You might think that Axiom 3 (the one about disjunctions) tells you to add up 100 probabilities $(\frac{1}{52} + \frac{1}{52} + \ldots + \frac{1}{52})$, but that can't be right; this sum exceeds 1, and the first axiom tells you that no probability can do that. In fact, Axiom 3 does not lead you astray; recall that it says that the probability of a disjunction is the sum of the probabilities of the disjunctions *when the disjuncts are incompatible with each other*; that ain't so in the present problem.

To do the right calculation, you need to rethink the problem. Set the *disjunction* aside and think instead about a *conjunction*: you don't get the ace of spades on the first draw, *and* you don't get it on the second, . . ., *and* you don't get it on the 100th. Since the draws are independent, the probability of *never* getting an ace of spades in 100 tries is $(\frac{51}{52})^{100}$, which is about 0.143. Each time you multiply a probability (that is strictly between 0 and 1) times itself, the product is smaller than the number with which you started. So the probability of getting at least one ace of spades in 100 tries is approximately $1 - 0.143 = 0.857$, which is pretty big. Improbable events have a big probability of happening if you try and try again.

This point can be put more carefully by distinguishing two propositions: (a) the single card dealt on this deal will be the ace of spades, and (b) at least one ace of spades will be dealt if you deal a single card, return it to the deck, reshuffle, and deal again, 100 times. It isn't true that (a) has a high probability if you do 100 deals. What is true is that (a) has a low probability and (b) has a high one.

2.3 Conditional Probability

Although I've said that probability assignments involve assumptions, I have yet to define the idea of *conditional* probability. I have talked about $Pr_A(H)$, not about $Pr_A(H \mid J)$. The latter represents the probability of H given J (where it is assumed that A is true). Take care to understand what this means. It doesn't say that J is true. The statement "if you toss the coin, then it will land heads" does not entail that you toss the coin; similarly, "Pr_A(the coin lands heads | you toss the coin) $= \frac{1}{2}$" does not say that you actually toss the coin. What it means is this: *suppose* that you have tossed the coin. You then are asked how probable it is that the coin will land heads, given that supposition. The value of the conditional probability is the answer to this question.

The concept of conditional probability is related as follows to the concept of unconditional probability that our axioms define:

$$Pr_A(H \mid J) = \frac{Pr_A(H \& J)}{Pr_A(J)}, \ \textit{if } Pr_A(J) > 0.$$

The equality in this conditional is called the **ratio formula**. Since you can't divide by zero, this "definition" of conditional probability offers no advice concerning what conditional probability means when $Pr_A(J) = 0$. I put "definition" in scare quotes because a (full) definition should provide necessary and sufficient conditions; the foregoing statement provides only the latter.

To understand why this "definition" of conditional probability makes sense, consider the ten objects described in Table 1. These objects are like pieces in a board game; some are square while others are circular, and some are green

Table 1 Each of ten objects has a color and a shape

	Green	Blue
Square	1	2
Circular	3	4

while others are blue. All four possible combinations of properties are represented in this collection. If you put these ten objects on your desk, close your eyes, and choose one at random, there is a $\frac{2}{10}$ chance that you'll choose a blue square, a $\frac{3}{10}$ chance you'll choose a green circle, and so on. These are each unconditional probabilities. But now consider how you would compute the probability that an object is green, given that it is square. There are three squares, and one of them is green, so the conditional probability is $\frac{1}{3}$. Another way to get this answer is to see that the probability that the piece is a green square is $\frac{1}{10}$ and the probability that it is a square is $\frac{3}{10}$, and $(\frac{1}{10})/(\frac{3}{10}) = \frac{1}{3}$. This calculation uses the ratio formula.

I use "assumption" to describe probability functions and "supposition" to describe conditional probabilities. These two terms sound like synonyms, but I am using them to pick out different things. Assumptions define probability functions whereas suppositions come up within a given probability function when a conditional probability is being evaluated. We often assemble assumptions that we believe are true and we often entertain suppositions that we don't think are true. I believe the deck is standard and that the cards are dealt at random. In contrast, I do not believe that the card you were just dealt is red, though I want to entertain that supposition to figure out the value of Pr(the card you are dealt is an ace | the card is red).

Although assumptions and suppositions are different, there is a numerical identity that connects them. If A and B are compatible, then

$$\mathrm{Pr}_{A\&B}(H) = \mathrm{Pr}_A(H \mid B).$$

The values are the same, but the epistemic status of B is subtly different.

How is the probability of a conjunction related to the probability of one of its conjuncts? The answer is that $\mathrm{Pr}_A(H\&J) \leq \mathrm{Pr}_A(J)$, no matter what A is. The concept of conditional probability can be used to explain why. Using the ratio formula, you can rewrite $\mathrm{Pr}_A(H\&J)$ as $\mathrm{Pr}_A(H \mid J)\mathrm{Pr}_A(J)$. From this you can see that $\mathrm{Pr}_A(H\&J) \leq \mathrm{Pr}_A(J)$. Since probabilities are numbers between 0 and 1, the product of two probabilities cannot be greater than the value of either of them. I hope this point strikes you as obvious, but it is anything but obvious to many people. In a much-cited psychology experiment, Tversky and Kahneman (1982b) told their subjects the following story:

> Linda is 31 years old, single, outspoken and very bright. She majored in philosophy. As a student, she was deeply concerned with issues of discrimination and social justice, and also participated in anti-nuclear demonstrations.

The subjects then were asked which of the following statements is more probable:

- Linda is a bank teller.
- Linda is a bank teller and is active in the feminist movement.

More than half the subjects in the experiment said that the second statement is more probable than the first. This example is a warning: when using the mathematical concept of probability, don't make the mistake of committing the "conjunction fallacy."

2.4 Bayes's Theorem

We now can use the ratio formula to derive the mathematical fact that goes by the name "Bayes's theorem." To simplify notation, I'll drop the subscript "A," but don't forget that a probability function is always based on assumptions! When I consider a conditional probability $\Pr(X \mid Y)$, I'll assume that $\Pr(Y) > 0$. And I'll now talk about propositions H and E, not propositions H and J, for a reason that soon will become clear.

Let's start by describing each of $\Pr(H \mid E)$ and $\Pr(E \mid H)$ in terms of ratios of unconditional probabilities:

$$\Pr(H \mid E) = \frac{\Pr(H\&E)}{\Pr(E)} \qquad \Pr(E \mid H) = \frac{\Pr(E\&H)}{\Pr(H)}$$

These two equations can be rearranged to yield:

$$\Pr(H\&E) = \Pr(H \mid E)\Pr(E) \qquad \Pr(E\&H) = \Pr(E \mid H)Pr(H)$$

The left-hand sides of these two equations are equal (since $H\&E$ is logically equivalent to $E\&H$), so the two right-hand sides must also be equal. Setting them equal and performing a little algebra yields:

Bayes's theorem: $\Pr(H \mid E) = \dfrac{\Pr(E \mid H)\Pr(H)}{\Pr(E)}.$

Bayes's theorem is true of any propositions H and E you please, but the typical application involves H being a "hypothesis" and E being "observational evidence."

In thinking about Bayes's theorem, it is important to recognize that $\Pr(H \mid E)$ and $\Pr(E \mid H)$ are different quantities and therefore may have different values. Much heartache will be avoided by attending to this difference! In logic it is a familiar fact that a conditional and its converse are different. For example, consider

- If noisy gremlins are bowling in your attic, then you hear noise coming from your attic.
- If you hear noise coming from your attic, then noisy gremlins are bowling in your attic.

It is obvious that the first can be true while the second is false. In just the same way, the following two conditional probabilities can have different values:

- Pr(you hear noise coming from your attic | noisy gremlins are bowling in your attic)
- Pr(noisy gremlins are bowling in your attic | you hear noise coming from your attic)

Personally, I think the first probability is big and the second is small.

The quantity $\Pr(E)$ on the right-hand side of Bayes's theorem deserves a comment. $\Pr(E)$ is the unconditional probability of the evidence E. In our gremlin example, E is the proposition that you hear noises coming from your attic. You might think that $\Pr(E)$ should be big if noises frequently come from up there and that it should be small if such noises are rare. This is sometimes right, but sometimes it isn't. To understand what the unconditional probability of E means, consider what the theorem of total probability says:

$$\Pr(E) = \Pr(E\&H) + \Pr(E\&notH).$$

Using the "definition" of conditional probability (and assuming that all the relevant probabilities are nonzero), we can rewrite this as

$$\Pr(E) = \Pr(E \mid H)\Pr(H) + \Pr(E \mid notH)\Pr(notH).^{10}$$

This shows why the value of $\Pr(E)$ will sometimes be very different from the frequency with which E is true. Consider the story about a world in which half the coins have two heads and half have two tails. You choose a coin at random and toss it repeatedly. Use the aforementioned equality to convince yourself that on each toss t, Pr(heads on toss t) = $\frac{1}{2}$. Yet, when you do the experiment, you obtain either 100% heads or 100% tails.[11]

2.5 Confirmation

Bayes's theorem follows from the axioms of probability and the "definition" of conditional probability. As such, it is not controversial. What is controversial is *Bayesianism*, which is the philosophical thesis that Bayes's theorem is the key to understanding claims about confirmation, evidence, rationality, and the goals of science.

I earlier defined probabilistic independence as a relationship among unconditional probabilities, but now let's express it by using the "definition" of

---

[10] More generally, if there are n mutually exclusive and collectively exhaustive hypotheses $(H_1, H_2, \ldots, H_n)$, then $\Pr(E) = \Pr(E \mid H_1)\Pr(H_1) + \Pr(E \mid H_2)\Pr(H_2) + \ldots + \Pr(E \mid H_n)\Pr(H_n) = \sum_i \Pr(E \mid H_i)\Pr(H_i)$.

[11] There's a *different* experiment that will probably yield around 50% heads if it has a large number of trials. Can you describe that experiment?

conditional probability. Recall that if hypothesis H and evidence E are probabilistically independent of each other, that means that

$\Pr(H\&E) = \Pr(H)\Pr(E)$.

If $\Pr(E) > 0$, this equality can be rewritten as

$\Pr(H \mid E) = \Pr(H)$,

which is equivalent to

$\Pr(H \mid E) = \Pr(H \mid notE)$.[12]

If H and E are probabilistically independent, whether E or *notE* is true makes no difference as far as the probability of H is concerned.

Turning now to the relationship of probabilistic *dependence*, we can state

The Bayesian definition of confirmation: Observation E confirms hypothesis H if and only if $\Pr(H \mid E) > \Pr(H)$.

Disconfirmation gets defined in tandem:

Observation E disconfirms hypothesis H if and only if $\Pr(H \mid E) < \Pr(H)$.[13]

Since assigning a value to $\Pr(H \mid E)$ does not require that E be true, the Bayesian definition of confirmation is better read as an explication of the following proposition: E, if true, would confirm H. A parallel point holds for disconfirmation.

Bayesianism entails that there is a symmetry between confirmation and disconfirmation:

E confirms H if and only if *notE* disconfirms H.

Convince yourself that this biconditional is correct when confirmation and disconfirmation are given Bayesian interpretations. Then use Bayes's theorem to convince yourself that confirmation is a symmetrical relation: if X confirms Y, then Y confirms X.

The Bayesian definition of confirmation can be used to underscore my earlier point that $\Pr(E)$ should not be defined as the frequency with which E is true. First notice that if $\Pr(E) = 1$, E cannot confirm the hypothesis H. Consult Bayes's theorem to see why this is true. Now suppose Susan takes numerous tuberculosis tests and they always come out positive. This might lead you to think that $\Pr(E) = 1$, where E says that Susan's test outcome is positive, but that

[12] To see why this equivalence holds, use the fact that $\Pr(H) = \Pr(H \mid E)\Pr(E) + \Pr(H \mid notE)\Pr(notE)$.
[13] Confirmational irrelevance is defined as $\Pr(H \mid E) = \Pr(H)$.

can't be right if the numerous positive outcomes confirm the hypothesis that Susan has tuberculosis.

2.6 Updating

The next distinctively Bayesian idea I need to describe concerns how agents should change their probability assignments as new evidence rolls in. All the probabilities described in Bayes's theorem use the same probability function, $\Pr_A()$. The assumptions in A can be thought of as the assumptions that an agent makes at a given time. Suppose you learn (with certainty) that a proposition N is true. Your set of assumptions has thereby been augmented. You need an *updating rule*, a rule that describes how the probabilities you assigned under your earlier probability function $\Pr_A()$ are related to the probabilities you should assign under your later probability function $\Pr_{A\&N}()$.

Before you are dealt a card from the standard deck of cards that I keep talking about, you think that $\Pr_A$(the card will be the ace of hearts | the card is red) $= \frac{1}{26}$. Suppose you then learn that the card is red. Call this new piece of information N; N gets added to what you already assumed, namely A. What value should you assign to $\Pr_{A\&N}$(the card will be the ace of hearts)? The *rule of updating by strict conditionalization* says your new unconditional probability should be $\frac{1}{26}$. More generally, the idea is this:

> **The Rule of Updating by Strict Conditionalization**: $\Pr_{t2}(H) = \Pr_{t1}(H \mid N)$ if the totality of what you learned between t_1 and t_2 is that N is true.

When you move from $\Pr_A(H \mid N)$ at t_1 to $\Pr_{A\&N}(H)$ at t_2, a supposition becomes an assumption.

This updating rule has two limitations. First, it characterizes learning as the discovery that some proposition N is true. However, if I tell you that N has a probability of, say, 0.6, the machinery of strict conditionalization doesn't tell you how to take this information into account.[14] Second, strict conditionalization describes how you should change your assignments of probability when you add a proposition to your assumptions, but it doesn't tell you what to do if something you previously assumed turns out to be false. The rule of strict conditionalization represents learning as gaining certainties, where a certainty, once gained, can never be lost.[15]

---

[14] Why not? Why not just define proposition N^* to mean that N has a probability of 0.6, and then compute the value of $\Pr(H \mid N^*)$? The problem is that one is then computing the probability of H conditional on a probability statement's being true. How is that supposed to work? One controversial answer is developed in Jeffrey (1965).

[15] Titelbaum (2013) develops a theory that aims to overcome this limitation.

I won't explore how these limitations of the strict conditionalization rule might be overcome. I introduce the rule because it allows me to explain some standard vocabulary. I have described $Pr_A(H)$ and $Pr_A(H \mid E)$ as the unconditional and the conditional probability of H, but it is customary to describe the former as H's *prior* probability and the latter as H's *posterior* probability. This temporal terminology is a bit misleading; it suggests that $Pr_A(H \mid E)$ is the probability assignment made after you learned that E is true, whereas $Pr_A(H)$ is the probability assignment made before. In fact, the A subscript means that both these probability assignments hold true under a single set of assumptions, and A might be the assumptions that an agent makes at a single time. Furthermore, don't forget that you don't need to believe E to assign a value of $Pr_A(H \mid E)$! What is true is that the value of the old conditional probability $Pr_A(H \mid E)$ is the same as the value of the new unconditional probability $Pr_{A\&E}(H)$ if E fully captured what you learned (and you use the rule of strict conditionalization). Don't let the temporal labels "posterior" and "prior" confuse you.

Bayes's theorem shows how gaining new information can lead you to change your degree of confidence in a hypothesis: this happens when the posterior probability has a different value from the prior. However, there are two cases in which no such change is possible. Bayes's theorem entails that if $Pr(H) = 0$ (or 1), then $Pr(H \mid E) = 0$ (or 1), no matter what E is; the two extreme probability values (0 and 1) are "sticky." This is why Bayesians usually are extremely cautious about assigning a hypothesis a prior (or a posterior!) of 0 or 1. Those assignments mean that no future experience should lead you to change your mind.

I talked about gremlins to illustrate the difference between $Pr(H \mid E)$ and $Pr(E \mid H)$. We now are calling the first of these H's posterior probability. The second also has a name – it is called H's *likelihood*. This terminology, due to R. A. Fisher, is unfortunate. In ordinary English, "probability" and "likelihood" are synonyms. In the technical parlance that now is canonical, they are not. To avoid confusing them, keep gremlins firmly in mind. When you hear noises in your attic, the gremlin hypothesis has a high likelihood but a low probability. From now on, when I say "likelihood," I'll be using the term's technical meaning.

2.7 The Odds Formulation of Bayes's Theorem

I now can complete my sketch of Bayesianism by describing an important consequence of Bayes's theorem. Suppose H_1 and H_2 are competing hypotheses. You want to know which of these hypotheses has the higher posterior probability, given your observational evidence E. If you write Bayes's theorem for each of these hypotheses, you can derive the following equation, which is called the *odds formulation of Bayes's theorem*:

$$\frac{\Pr(H_1 \mid E)}{\Pr(H_2 \mid E)} = \frac{\Pr(E \mid H_1)}{\Pr(E \mid H_2)} \frac{\Pr(H_1)}{\Pr(H_2)}.$$

This says that the ratio of posterior probabilities equals the likelihood ratio multiplied by the ratio of prior probabilities. Notice that the unconditional probability of the observations, $\Pr(E)$, has disappeared. The odds formulation says that there is exactly one way that an observation E can lead you to change how confident you are in H_1 as compared with H_2. If the ratio of posteriors is to differ from the ratio of priors, this must be because the likelihoods differ.

The odds formulation of Bayes's theorem makes it easy to see how a hypothesis with a very low prior probability can have its probability driven above 0.5 by several favorable observations, even when one such observation is not enough to do so. Consider Susan and her positive tuberculosis test. Suppose the prior probability of Susan's having tuberculosis is 0.001. She then takes a tuberculosis test that has the following properties:

Pr(positive test outcome | Susan has tuberculosis) = 0.96
Pr(positive test outcome | Susan does not have tuberculosis) = 0.02.[16]

Let's use the odds formulation of Bayes's theorem to compute the ratio of posterior probabilities from the numbers just stated. The likelihood ratio is 48. The ratio of the priors is $\frac{1}{999}$. So the ratio of the posterior probabilities is $\frac{48}{999}$. This last number means that the posterior probability of Susan's having tuberculosis is $\frac{48}{999+48}$.[17] This is far less than $\frac{1}{2}$, but bigger than $\frac{1}{1000}$. The positive test result increased Susan's probability of having tuberculosis, but not enough to drive that probability above $\frac{1}{2}$. Now suppose that Susan takes the test a second time and again gets a positive result. Since the two test results are independent of each other, conditional on each of the two hypotheses, the odds formulation of Bayes's theorem will take the following form:

$$\frac{\Pr(H_1 \mid E_1 \& E_2)}{\Pr(H_2 \mid E_1 \& E_2)} = \frac{\Pr(E_2 \mid H_1)}{\Pr(E_2 \mid H_2)} \frac{\Pr(E_1 \mid H_1)}{\Pr(E_1 \mid H_2)} \frac{\Pr(H_1)}{\Pr(H_2)}.$$

The product of the two likelihood ratios is $(48)(48) = 2{,}304$. Given the ratio of the priors, the ratio of the posterior probabilities is now $\frac{2304}{999}$, so the probability of tuberculosis is now $\frac{2304}{999+2304}$, which is about 0.69. The *single* positive test outcome does not entail that Susan probably has the disease, but the *two*

---

[16] Notice that these two probabilities don't sum to 1. $\Pr(A \mid B) + \Pr(notA \mid B)$ must sum to 1, but $\Pr(A \mid B)$ and $\Pr(A \mid notB)$ need not; the sum can be more than 1 as well as less than 1.

[17] This follows from the fact that $\frac{p}{(1-p)} = \frac{48}{999}$, where p = Pr(Susan has tuberculosis | positive test outcome).

positive outcomes do. People often think that if they take a reliable tuberculosis test and get a positive outcome, then they probably have tuberculosis.[18] Tversky and Kahneman (1982a) call this *the fallacy of base rate neglect*; the mistake is the failure to take account of prior probabilities.

2.8 The Law of Likelihood

When I introduced the odds version of Bayes's theorem, I mentioned that the likelihood ratio is the sole vehicle in the Bayesian framework whereby new evidence can modify your relative confidence in competing hypotheses. It will be useful to have a principle that isolates this unique role. Hacking (1965) calls the following the *law of likelihood*:

> *Evidence E favors hypothesis H_1 over hypothesis H_2 if and only if $Pr(E \mid H_1) > Pr(E \mid H_2)$.*

When the evidence favors H_1 over H_2 in this sense, the ratio of posterior probabilities exceeds the ratio of priors.

What justifies the law of likelihood? Unlike Bayes's theorem, it isn't a deductive consequence of the axioms of probability and the "definition" of conditional probability. This is because the concept of *favoring* isn't used in the axioms of probability. So perhaps we should regard the law as a clarification of what the word "favoring" means in ordinary language. If we do so, we must conclude that the law is flawed. Suppose a talented weather forecaster looks at today's weather conditions and concludes that there probably will be snow tomorrow. The forecaster might summarize this finding by saying that the present weather conditions favor snow tomorrow over no snow tomorrow. Here the word "favoring" is used to describe an inequality between *posterior probabilities*, not a *likelihood* inequality; the claim is that

> Pr(snow tomorrow | today's weather conditions) > Pr(no snow tomorrow | today's weather conditions).

Thus, if the law of likelihood is supposed to describe what "favoring" means, it is false (Sober 2008). An alternative interpretation of the law of likelihood is better. We can regard the law as a stipulation; the term "favoring" is being used to mark the fact that likelihood inequalities have a special evidential significance (as revealed by the odds formulation of Bayes's theorem), with no

---

[18] I say the test is reliable when its two error probabilities – Pr(S's test result is negative | S has tuberculosis) and Pr(S's test result is positive | S does not have tuberculosis) – are small. This does not mean that Pr(S has tuberculosis | S's test result is negative) and Pr(S does not have tuberculosis | S's test result is positive) are small! As with gremlins, the distinction between Pr(X | Y) and Pr(Y | X) is vital.

pretense that the law perfectly captures what "favoring" means in ordinary English.[19] It is not for nothing that Bayesians call the likelihood ratio "the Bayes factor."[20]

It is a consequence of the law of likelihood that the evidence at hand may favor an implausible hypothesis over a sensible one. When you observe that the card you are dealt is an ace, the law says that this observation favors the hypothesis that the deck is made entirely of aces over the hypothesis that the deck is normal (since $1 > \frac{4}{52}$). This may sound like a decisive objection to the law, but there is a reply. Your doubts about the first hypothesis stem from information you had before you observed the ace, not from what you just observed (Edwards 1972; Royall 1997). Likelihood comparisons are supposed to isolate what the evidence says, not to settle which hypotheses are more plausible overall.

The law of likelihood allows that an observation can favor one hypothesis over another even when neither hypothesis predicts the observation. Suppose $\Pr(E \mid H_1) = 0.4$ and $\Pr(E \mid H_2) = 0.001$. Neither hypothesis "predicts" E in the sense of saying that E is more probable than not; yet E discriminates between the two hypotheses. Asking what a hypothesis "predicts" is a highly imperfect guide to interpreting evidence.

I earlier described a symmetry that connects confirmation and disconfirmation: If E confirms H, then *notE* disconfirms H. There also is a symmetry that follows from the law of likelihood: if E favors H_1 over H_2, then *notE* favors H_2 over H_1.[21]

2.9 The Principle of Total Evidence

The law of likelihood tells you how to use observations to evaluate hypotheses, but there are many true descriptions of what you observe. This raises the question of which of those true descriptions you should use. For example, suppose the urn before you contains a large number of balls, each of which is either red or green. You close your eyes, reach into the urn, and remove 100 balls. You want to evaluate two competing hypotheses:

---

[19] Stipulations are often said to be "arbitrary." However, within the Bayesian framework, there is nothing arbitrary about the claim that the likelihood ratio plays a special epistemic role. What is a bit arbitrary is using the word "favoring" to name that role. This example reveals one limitation of the idea that philosophy's sole aim is to explicate concepts that already have names in ordinary language.

[20] Fitelson (2011) argues that Bayesians should reject the law of likelihood. Forster (2006) provides a non-Bayesian criticism of the law, as do Vassend, Sober, and Fitelson (2017). Zhang and Zhang (2015) reply to Forster. For further discussion of the law's justification, see Royall (1997), Forster and Sober (2004), and Sober (2008, pp. 32–38).

[21] Warning: if E_1 and E_2 are incompatible, it isn't true that E_1 favors H_1 over H_2 precisely when E_2 favors H_2 over H_1. What is true is that if $E_1, E_2, \ldots, E_n$ are exclusive and exhaustive, then if E_i favors H_1 over H_2, then there exists at least one E_j $(j \neq i)$ that favors H_2 over H_1.

(H1)   80% of the balls in the urn are green and 20% are red.

(H2)   30% of the balls in the urn are green and 70% are red.

Suppose you observe that ninety of the balls sampled are green and ten are red. Using the law of likelihood, you conclude that this evidence (call it E_s) favors H_1 over H_2, since

$$\Pr(E_s \mid H_1) > \Pr(E_s \mid H_2).$$

So far so good, but now notice that if you used a different true description of your observations, you would reach a different verdict. Each of the balls you observed was either green or red; call this observation statement E_w. E_w does not favor either hypothesis over the other, since

$$\Pr(E_w \mid H_1) = \Pr(E_w \mid H_2).$$

The inequality and the equality just described are both true, and both use true descriptions of what you observed, but these descriptions lead to different evaluations of the two hypotheses. Which should you use? Here's a principle that provides an answer:

> **The Principle of Total Evidence:** When evaluating whether your evidence favors one hypothesis over another, use the logically strongest true description of your evidence on which each of the hypotheses confers a probability.[22]

E_s is logically stronger than E_w (in the technical sense of that term), because E_s entails E_w, but not conversely. E_w has thrown away relevant information, since it induces a likelihood equality while E_s yields an inequality. The principle of total evidence tells you to use E_s rather than E_w when you test H_1 against H_2.

2.10 Likelihoodism

To keep things simple, I discussed the law of likelihood in terms of its role in the odds formulation of Bayes's theorem. However, there is a philosophy of probability that sees the law of likelihood as having merit on its own; making it part of a larger, Bayesian picture isn't necessary and is often undesirable. I call this view *likelihoodism*. Here's an example. When Arthur Stanley Eddington observed the bending of light during a solar eclipse in 1919, this observation was widely taken to provide compelling evidence favoring Einstein's general

---

[22] This version of the principle of total evidence is a bit nonstandard, in that a Bayesian version will usually concern posterior probabilities, enjoining you to conditionalize on all the evidence you have. The Bayesian and likelihood versions of this principle are joined at the hip by the odds formulation of Bayes's theorem.

theory of relativity over the classical physics of Newton. Likelihoodists represent this in terms of the following inequality:

Pr(Eddington's data on the solar eclipse | general relativity theory) >
Pr(Eddington's data on the solar eclipse | classical mechanics).

You don't need to think about the prior probability of either theory to see that this inequality is true. Furthermore, likelihoodists see no way to justify an assignment of prior probabilities to general relativity and classical mechanics. True, you may have some subjective degree of confidence in each of these hypotheses, but someone else may have a different degree of confidence, and there is no way to decide who is right. When this is true, likelihoodists foreswear prior probabilities,[23] and this means that they don't assign values to the posterior probabilities of these two theories, either. The claim that scientists ought to figure out how probable various theories are may sound like a truism, but likelihoodism disagrees.[24]

One traditional strategy for assigning values to prior probabilities is to appeal to the *principle of indifference*. This principle says that if $H_1, H_2, \ldots, H_n$ are exclusive and exhaustive hypotheses, and you have no reason to think that one of them is more probable than any of the others, you should assign the same probability to each, namely $\frac{1}{n}$. The principle says that probabilities can be obtained from ignorance. Unless restricted, it leads to contradiction. Consider "God exists" and "God does not exist" and suppose you have no reason to think one more probable than the other. The result is that each gets assigned a probability of $\frac{1}{2}$. But now consider the triplet "God exists and Christianity is true," "God exists and Christianity is false," and "God does not exist." If you don't have reason to think that one of these is more probable than the others, you assign each a probability of $\frac{1}{3}$, with the result that "God exists" receives a probability of $\frac{2}{3}$. You now have contradicted yourself. This is why many Bayesians eschew the principle of indifference.[25]

---

[23] You can see here why likelihoodists don't like the "definition" of conditional probability as a ratio of unconditional probabilities. Likelihoodists think that likelihoods often make sense when priors do not.

[24] So does frequentism, a varied collection of ideas that includes significance tests, Neyman-Pearson hypothesis testing, confidence intervals, and model selection criteria like AIC and cross-validation.

[25] Can the objection to Bayesianism that focuses on its need for prior probabilities be dealt with by appeal to theorems concerning "the washing out of priors"? The idea here is that agents who start with very different prior probabilities and then interpret the evidence in the same way (because they agree on the values of the likelihoods) will end up agreeing on the posterior probabilities; their different starting points don't matter in the long run. The mathematical arguments appealed to here are correct, but the problem is that they are asymptotic (meaning that they are about what happens in the limit). When agents who have different priors confront a finite data set, they will disagree about the posteriors, often dramatically; what would happen

Another strategy for assigning values to prior probabilities is better. If you want a prior probability for Susan's having tuberculosis, it may make sense to use the frequency of tuberculosis in Wisconsin, if all you know about Susan is that she lives in Wisconsin. Using frequencies to estimate probabilities in this case seems reasonable.[26] Unfortunately, this strategy doesn't allow you to obtain a defensible prior for general relativity; you can't sample universes and compute the frequency with which they obey that theory.

Although likelihoodists aren't Bayesians, there is a formal connection between the law of likelihood and Bayesian confirmation theory:

$\Pr(E \mid H) > \Pr(E \mid notH)$ if and only if $\Pr(H \mid E) > \Pr(H)$.

E favors H over $notH$ (in the sense of the law of likelihood) precisely when E confirms H (in the sense of Bayesianism). You can use Bayes's theorem to prove this biconditional. Does this formal connection show that likelihoodists are Bayesians under the skin? No. In addition to eschewing prior probabilities, likelihoodists think that assigning a value to $\Pr(E \mid notH)$ often lacks an objective justification. It is clear enough what the probability was of Eddington's observations of the solar eclipse, given general relativity. However, the probability of those observations, given the *negation* of general relativity, is utterly opaque. The negation of general relativity is a vast disjunction, covering all possible alternatives to general relativity, including ones that have not yet been formulated. The likelihood of *notGTR* therefore takes the following form:

$$\Pr(O \mid notGTR) = \sum_i \Pr(O \mid A_i)\Pr(A_i \mid notGTR).$$

The likelihood of *notGTR* is a weighted average of the likelihoods of all the alternatives (the A_i's) to *GTR*; to compute this average, you need to know how probable each A_i is, given *notGTR*. Philosophers of science call the negation of general relativity a "catchall hypothesis" (Shimony 1970). Likelihoodists restrict their epistemology to "specific" theories – to general relativity and Newtonian mechanics, for example. So there are *two* reasons why likelihood-ists aren't Bayesians: they often don't want to talk about the prior and posterior probabilities of theories *and* they often don't want to talk about the likelihoods of catchalls (Sober 2008).

It may be helpful to distinguish Bayesianism from likelihoodism by using the distinction between *private* and *public*. Bayesianism is a philosophy for indi-vidual agents who want to decide how confident they should be in various

---

in the infinite long run doesn't change that point. Think about Susan's one or two tuberculosis tests.

[26] For this reason, likelihoodism, as I use that term, doesn't claim that *all* prior probabilities are illegitimate.

hypotheses.[27] Likelihoodism is an epistemology for the social world of science; it aims to isolate something objective on which agents can agree, whether or not they agree about how probable the hypotheses under consideration are. Individuals may need prior and posterior probabilities to live their lives, but science needs something that transcends individual differences.

Bayesians often think of probabilities in terms of the subjective degrees of belief that agents have or should have. Likelihoodists usually prefer to view the probabilities they use as being about an objective mind-independent reality. It is an objective fact about Einstein's theory and classical mechanics that Eddington's observations are more probable under the former than they are under the latter. The same holds for the hypotheses and observations in the urn example discussed earlier.

Bayesians differ among themselves, but they tend to agree that *computing the posterior probabilities of hypotheses is always an attainable goal.* Likelihoodists claim that this goal is often impossible to achieve. They hold that when Bayesianism fails, discovering which of several specific hypotheses the evidence favors is often an attainable goal. Likelihoodism's goal is more modest than Bayesianism's. In a sense, likelihoodism is an *attenuated* Bayesianism; likelihoodism is what remains of Bayesianism when some of the latter is stripped away.

3 Six Ways to Formulate a Design Argument

In Section 1, I briefly discussed design arguments that seek to deduce the conclusion that God exists. Here, I focus on nondeductive design arguments. These have taken different forms; they have been nearly deductive, inductive, analogical, Bayesian, likelihoodist, and abductive. In each case, the argument has a structure that is supposed to apply to theological and nontheological subject matters alike. That comes with the territory, since design arguments are part of *natural* theology.

My list of possible forms of argument may give the impression that I think that each is okay, and that my only question will be whether a given design argument measures up. Not so! Design arguments sometimes go wrong by buying into styles of argumentation that are flawed. Echoing a wry analogy of Bertrand Russell's (1912), I suggest that some of these argument forms are "relics of a bygone age, surviving, like the monarchy, only because they are

---

[27] Howson and Urbach (1993) make the good point that Bayesianism isn't obliged to tell agents what their prior probabilities should be, any more than deductive logic is obliged to tell agents what their premises should be. However, my point about priors isn't about the duties of Bayesianism, but about its usefulness in some epistemic contexts.

erroneously supposed to do no harm." My goal in this section is to identify the strongest form a design argument can take. It is time to sift and winnow.

3.1 Nearly Deductive

In statistics, a *significance test* tells you to reject a hypothesis (i.e., regard it as false) if the hypothesis says that the probability of your observation is sufficiently low. For example, you can test the hypothesis that a coin is fair (that its probability of heads on each toss is $\frac{1}{2}$) by tossing the coin twenty times and seeing how often it lands heads. If the coin is fair, its probability of producing either 0–4 heads or 16–20 heads is less than 0.05. If the outcome of your experiment falls into that disjunctive region, you reject the hypothesis at the 0.05 level of significance. If the outcome does not fall in that "rejection region," you decline to reject.[28]

In this significance test, you consider the probability that the outcome falls into a disjunctive region, not the probability of the outcome's having its observed point value. The disjunctive formulation is needed if significance tests are to avoid an absurd consequence. The probability of getting *exactly* 200 heads, if you toss a fair coin 400 times, is only 0.04, and each of the other possible point outcomes has an even lower probability. If your policy is to reject the hypothesis that the coin is fair when the probability of the point outcome is less than 0.05, you'll reject the hypothesis no matter what frequency you observe, which is absurd. This is why a disjunctive "rejection region" is used. The practice is to single out the relevant disjunction by taking the observed point frequency and lumping it together with others that the hypothesis under test says are no more probable.[29]

Suppose Susan gets a negative test result when she takes a tuberculosis test, and Pr(Susan's test result is negative | Susan has tuberculosis) < 0.05. Do the rules of significance testing say that you can reject the hypothesis that Susan has tuberculosis at the 0.05 level? The answer is *yes*. The rules say to construct a rejection region that includes the actual outcome and all the possible outcomes that are no more probable than the one that occurred. This rule applies to the tuberculosis test just as it does to the coin. The logic is the same, whether there are two possible outcomes, or twenty-one.

---

[28] Significance tests require a single hypothesis to say how probable an observation is, but do not ask a second, competing hypothesis to do the same. For example, a significance test of "the coin is fair" does not require you to say how probable your observations would be if the coin were *un*fair. Significance tests are not *contrastive*, unlike Neyman-Pearson hypothesis tests, and the Bayesian and likelihoodist ideas I discuss.

[29] There are other ways to define a disjunctive rejection region, and no rationale, except "naturalness," for focusing on the one that is customary (Howson and Urbach, 1993, pp. 182–183).

I say (with tongue in cheek) that significance test arguments are "nearly" deductive because the following two argument forms look similar:

If H, then $notE$.
E
_____
$notH$

If H, then probably $notE$.
E
_____
$notH$

The left-hand argument (*modus tollens*) is deductively valid, so the right-hand argument (which could be called "probabilistic *modus tollens*") may seem to make sense because it approximates the deductive ideal.[30] I will argue that this impression is mistaken.

Significance testing has been harnessed in design arguments for the existence of God. Here's an example:

We observe that object o has characteristic C.
Pr(o has C | o obtained its features by the process of natural selection) is very small.

_____

We should reject the hypothesis that o obtained C by the process of natural selection.

Rejecting the hypothesis of natural selection, of course, does not license accepting the God hypothesis. As noted in Section 1, a mindless process other than natural selection may have been responsible. However, if God and natural selection are the only known alternatives, rejecting one of them leaves just one known alternative standing.

Design arguments of this sort inherit the general problems that beset significance tests. The first is that the choice of 0.05 as one's level of significance is conventional; it is arbitrary to say how low $\Pr(E \mid H)$ must be for E to justify rejecting H. A second problem is that it often makes no sense to reject a hypothesis just because it says that an observation is very improbable. Your winning the lottery had a probability of $\frac{1}{1,000,000}$ according to the hypothesis that the lottery was fair and a million tickets were sold, but that isn't enough for you to reject the hypothesis (Sober 2002, 2012).

There's a third reason why you shouldn't reject a hypothesis just because it says that your observations were very improbable. Suppose you test hypothesis H by doing n different experiments; in each, there is one outcome that H says is very probable and 100 that H says are very improbable. You do the experiments

_____

[30] It might seem that I should have written "probably $notH$" as the conclusion of the right-hand argument, but that is not how significance tests work. They do not assign probabilities to hypotheses; they aren't Bayesian. Even so, it is worth recalling the distinction between $\Pr(E \mid H)$ and $\Pr(H \mid E)$. The fact that the former is low doesn't entail that the latter is (§2.4).

and in each case the outcome that H says is very probable is the one that comes to pass. This sounds like very good news for hypothesis H, but consider this: even though H assigns a *high* probability to each of E_1, E_2, ..., E_n, it can turn out that H says that the *conjunction* of those n events is very improbable. This happens when H assigns a probability less than one to each event, the events are sufficiently numerous, and they are probabilistically independent of each other, conditional on H. The conjunction of the E_i's counts as an observation just as much as each conjunct does. If your policy is to reject a theory when it says that your observations are very improbable, you will reject every probabilistic theory that makes 100% successful predictions! This shows that the policy is absurd.

The lottery example makes it seem obvious that significance tests are wrong to conclude that a hypothesis is false just because it says that an observation was very improbable. However, this feeling of obviousness can fade when you look at examples in which the relevant probability is much smaller than $\frac{1}{1,000,000}$. Henry Morris (1980) says that if event E occurs, any theory that assigns E a probability less than $\frac{1}{10^{110}}$ should be rejected. Morris chooses this cut-off because 10^{110} is his estimate of the number of times elementary particles could have changed state since the universe began.

Morris is a creationist, but it isn't just creationists who embrace this form of argument. Richard Dawkins (1986, pp. 143–146), an atheist and a biologist, does so as well when he considers what a respectable theory of the origin of life on Earth is permitted to assert:

> [T]here are some levels of sheer luck, not only too great for puny human imaginations, but too great to be allowed in our hard-headed calculations about the origin of life. But ... how great a level of luck, how much of a miracle, *are* we allowed to postulate? ... The answer ... depends upon whether our planet is the only one that has life, or whether life abounds all around the universe. ... [T]he maximum amount of luck that we are allowed to assume, before we reject a particular theory of the origin of life, has odds of one in N, where N is the number of suitable planets in the universe. There is a lot hidden in that word "suitable" but let us put an upper limit of 1 in 100 billion billion for the maximum amount of luck that this argument entitles us to assume.

We now know of just one planet (our own) on which life exists, so if there are N suitable planets, the frequency of life in those suitable planets is at least $\frac{1}{N}$. Dawkins takes that to mean that a theory of the origin of life on Earth must say that the *probability* of that event is at least $\frac{1}{N}$. To evaluate Dawkins's suggestion, we need to consider how actual frequency and probability are related. With a small sample size, it is perfectly possible for these quantities to have very different values; consider a fair coin that is tossed three times and then destroyed. The probability that it lands heads is $\frac{1}{2}$, but the frequency of heads might well be zero or one. However, when sample size is very large, the actual frequency often provides a good estimate of the probability. Dawkins tells you to reject a theory if the probability it assigns to an event is too *low*, but why doesn't he also say that you should reject it if the probability it assigns is too *high*? The reason, presumably, is that you cannot rule out the possibility that planet Earth was not just suitable but *highly conducive* to the evolution of life. However, this point cuts both ways. Even if $\frac{1}{N}$ is a good estimate of the *average* probability that life will evolve on a suitable planet, different suitable planets may have different probabilities; some planets may have values that are greater than $\frac{1}{N}$ while others may have values that are lower. Dawkins's lower bound assumes *a priori* that our planet was either average or above average in its life-conduciveness. This mistake might be termed the "Lake Wobegon Fallacy."[31]

I said that significance tests involve a decision about whether to reject a hypothesis, but there are two other interpretations to consider (Royall 1997). R. A. Fisher (1956, pp. 39, 43), who invented significance tests, says that when event E happens and $\Pr(E \mid H)$ is low, you should conclude that either H is false or something very improbable has occurred. If Fisher is right, design arguments go wrong when they deploy rejectionist significance tests.[32] The other interpretation says that E counts as evidence against H when $\Pr(E \mid H)$ is low enough. This conflicts with the law of likelihood (§2.8), a point I return to later in this section.

William Dembski (1998a) and Stephen Meyer (2009), who are intelligent design proponents, take significance tests as their point of departure, but they recognize that a low value for Pr(o has C | o has its characteristics owing to natural selection) does not suffice for the observation to justify rejecting the hypothesis. However, when the probability is low and characteristic C is "specified," they think you should reject. Dembski's concept of specification is technical and intricate; for criticisms, see Fitelson, Stephens, and Sober (1999). Meyer (2009, p. 185) describes Dembski's idea like this: "*o*'s having C exhibits a specified pattern" means that we independently know that *o*'s having C performs a function or advances a goal. This gloss of Dembski's idea suggests that he is still in the world of significance tests; the claim is that we should reject the hypothesis of natural selection when it says that the probability is very low that an organism will have a given functional feature.

---

[31] In Lake Wobegon, a fictional town created by Garrison Keillor for his *Prairie Home Companion* radio show, "all the women are strong, all the men are good looking, and all the children are above average."

[32] Fisher's disjunction is sometimes wrong. Suppose that $\Pr(E \mid H)$ is very low and that $\Pr(E \mid H^*)$ is high, where H^* is true and entails H. This shows that there are *three* possibilities to consider: either H is false, or something improbable has happened, or H is true but incomplete.

This is just a restricted significance test, and inherits the defects of the unrestricted concept.

Dembski (1998a) and Meyer (2009, p. 355) make a further claim: an event that exhibits specified complexity[33] (complexity is their term for low probability) licenses rejecting *all* possible mindless processes; you don't need to consider such hypotheses one by one. Here the significance test idea is left behind and is replaced by Dembski's "explanatory filter." This protocol involves a sequence of decisions:

(1) If an event E has a high probability, you should accept the hypothesis that it is due to necessity or natural law; otherwise you should reject that hypothesis and move down the list.

(2) If E has a middling probability, or has a low probability and is unspecified, you should accept the hypothesis that it is due to chance; otherwise you should reject that hypothesis and move down the list.

(3) If E has a low probability and is specified, it is due to intelligent design.

Notice that the filter focuses on the unconditional probability of E, not on the probability of E conditional on some hypothesis. Significance tests aren't like this, and neither are the Bayesian and likelihoodist design arguments that I will soon describe. Recall from §2.4 that the unconditional probability of observation E is the average probability of E under all possible hypotheses, weighted by the probabilities of those hypotheses; the value of this quantity is often unknowable. In addition, Dembski's framework has a peculiar consequence: if you observe that O_1 and O_2 are both true, and O_1 has a high probability and O_2 has a probability that is middling, then no hypothesis can explain them both.

3.2 Inductive Sampling

Although you did not observe me writing the page before you, you have seen intelligent designers write other such pages, and those observations seem to license a conclusion about this one. The structure of this bit of reasoning is as follows:

All (or nearly all) of the many events that have characteristic C, whose causes we *have* observed, were observed to have been caused by the intentional activity of an intelligent designer.

(BI) ——————————————————

Probably, all (or nearly all) of the many events that have characteristic C, whose causes we have *not* observed, were caused by the intentional activity of an intelligent designer.

---

[33] Meyer (2009, p. 107) says that his concept of specified information is equivalent to Dembski's concept of specified complexity.

I call this argument "BI" because it involves a *backward* induction; you observe objects that have characteristic C and trace them back in time to observe their causes.[34]

A BI argument surfaces in Hume's 1779 *Dialogues Concerning Natural Religion*.[35] Cleanthes, a character in the *Dialogues*, says in Part 3 that if we heard an "articulate voice from the clouds" speaking to each of us in his or her own language, and delivering to each of us a message "altogether worthy of a benevolent Being, superior to mankind," we should conclude that these sounds were produced intentionally by an intelligent agent. Cleanthes's point is that when we have observed the causes of utterances in human languages, those causes always turned out to be intelligent beings intentionally producing those utterances, so when this voice comes to us from the sky, we should infer that it has the same type of cause.

Though Cleanthes's *conclusion* about the voice seems sensible, the BI *form of argument* is problematic. BI arguments focus exclusively on the causes we have *actually* observed; it ignores causes that may have operated before human beings existed, or that may have operated far away in space, or that may have occurred too slowly for human beings to notice. The inductive sampling version of the design argument is *biased* against theories that postulate unobservable processes; it commits to an over-narrow empiricism.

Critics of the design argument sometimes make the same mistake. Philo, another character in the *Dialogues*, criticizes a design argument concerning "the origin of worlds." In Part 2, he notes that we have never visited other universes and seen intelligent designers bring them into being; he concludes that the cosmic design argument is as weak as weak can be. Philo's argument has an unfortunate consequence; it entails that modern physics is on a fool's errand when it theorizes about the origin of the universe. But Philo is wrong; physicists are able to muster evidence for the Big Bang hypothesis even though they have never observed other universes coming into existence.

What happens if the biological design argument is given a BI formulation? When you look at the adaptive features of organisms and trace their causes back in time, you *rarely* observe intelligent designers intentionally producing the features you observe. What you mostly see is ancestors reproducing without intending that their progeny have adaptive features. Friends of the design

---

[34] In Section 4, I discuss the idea of *forward*-inductive sampling. There you look at known intelligent designers and observe the kinds of artifacts they intentionally produce.

[35] For discussion of Hume's *Dialogues* that goes beyond what I can cover here, see O'Connor (2001), Pyle (2006), and Sober (forthcoming-a).

argument think this is true because you have not pushed your inquiry far enough back; if you were to do this, they think, you would eventually come to one or more intelligent designers. Of course that *is* what creationists believe, but this comment evades the demands that the inductive sampling argument imposes. When you look backward in time at the causal histories of watches, computers, and paintings, you observe the intentional production of adaptive features, but when you do the same for wombats, chameleons, and petunias, you do not. The first group does not outnumber the second, so a BI argument based on this sample should lead you to conclude that it is *not* probable that objects with adaptive features, whose causes you have not observed, were intentionally caused.[36] Philo makes this point in Section 7 of Hume's *Dialogues* (Salmon 1978).

I hope you won't conclude from this section that I am "against induction." If you draw 100 balls at random from an urn that contains 10,000 balls, and observe that 60 of the 100 are green, the maximum likelihood estimate of the frequency of green balls in the urn is 60%. Your observation favors this estimate over others in the sense of the law of likelihood. If you have a justified prior probability distribution concerning the urn's composition, you can compute the posterior probability that the urn's frequency of green balls is about 60%. Both likelihoodism and Bayesianism allow that there are good inductive arguments. However, the BI design argument isn't one of them.

3.3 Analogical

Analogical arguments infer that a target object t has characteristic C because an analog object a is observed to have C, and t and a are seen to be similar. Analogical design arguments are a species of that genus:

Target object t and analog object a are observed to be similar to degree p.
We observe that a was intentionally created by an intelligent designer.
$p[\rule{3cm}{0.4pt} $

Object t was intentionally created by an intelligent designer.

---

[36] Behe (2004, p. 355), a friend of the design argument, says that "the logical structure of the argument to design is a simple inductive one: whenever we see such highly specific interactions in our everyday world, whether in a mousetrap or elsewhere, we unfailingly find that the systems were intentionally arranged – that they were designed. Now we find systems of similar complexity in the cell. Since no other explanation has successfully addressed them, I argue that we should extend the induction to subsume molecular machines, and hypothesize that they were purposely designed." Meyer (2009) sometimes endorses a design argument based on BI sampling; for example, he says that "our experience of the world shows that what we recognize as information invariably reflects the activity of conscious and intelligent persons" (p. 16) and "we know from experience that only conscious, intelligent agents produce large amounts of specified information" (p. 429). Elsewhere Meyer (p. 347) characterizes his design argument as an inference to the best explanation. I discuss that style of argument later in this section.

Notice that "p" occurs twice in this argument. It represents the degree of observed similarity between analog and target, and it also represents the probability that the premises confer on the conclusion (Sober 1993).

In Part 12.7 of the *Dialogues*, Hume has Philo object to an analogical design argument. Using the format just described, he notes that human artifacts (e.g., a watch) and the whole universe are different in numerous respects; Philo concludes that the design argument's conclusion (that the universe was made by an intelligent designer) is improbable, since the analogy is "remote."

The main defect in this form of argument is that it assumes that every observed "match" between target and analog has the same impact on probabilities, and it gives an observed match and an observed mismatch equal weight. If you assess target and analog for each of ten features, and they match on just one, the degree of observed similarity is $\frac{1}{10}$, and that is said to be the probability of intelligent design. It doesn't matter which characteristic is doing the matching and which ones furnish the mismatches. Watches go tick-tock and are made of metal and glass; the vertebrate eye is silent and is made of flesh and blood. Do each of these mismatches undermine the design hypothesis to the same degree that the functional delicacy of watches and eyes confirms it? In Part 2.9 of the *Dialogues*, Hume has Cleanthes, the defender of the design argument, say *no*, as well he should.

This defect in the analogical formulation of the design argument is also visible when you consider two objects that were both intelligently designed, but you observe that they are very different. A thumbtack and the international space station are very dissimilar, yet it would be a mistake to conclude that the thumbtack's being intelligently designed makes it very improbable that the space station is too.[37]

The difficulties for analogy arguments that I've described can be circumvented by replacing overall similarity with the following principle: "to the same natural effects we must, as far as possible, assign the same causes." Given this principle, the delicate functionality of a watch and the delicate functionality of the vertebrate eye allow you to conclude that the eye was produced by an intelligent designer since the watch was. This principle has a glorious history; it was Newton's second rule of reasoning, which he put in the second edition of his *Principia*. Unfortunately, the prestige of Newton's physics rubbed off on his dubious principle. The trouble is, similar effects are often best explained by postulating *dissimilar* causes. For example, fire engines are red and so are

---

[37] My thanks to Sean Liebowitz for this example.

roses.[38] In addition, the proviso "as far as possible" puts the principle in peril of being vacuous.[39]

3.4 Bayesian

If you observe that object o has characteristic C, a Bayesian design argument seeks to show that this observation makes it probable (i.e., probability $> \frac{1}{2}$) that God exists. The odds formulation of Bayes's theorem (§2.7) describes what this Bayesian argument needs to establish:

$$\frac{\Pr(God\ exists\ |\ o\ has\ C)}{\Pr(God\ does\ not\ exist\ |\ o\ has\ C)} = \frac{\Pr(o\ has\ C\ |\ God\ exists)}{\Pr(o\ has\ C\ |\ God\ does\ not\ exist)}$$
$$\times\ \frac{\Pr(God\ exists)}{\Pr(God\ does\ not\ exist)}.$$

To see whether the left-hand ratio is greater than one, you need to consider the likelihood ratio and the ratio of prior probabilities on the right.

This Bayesian argument needs to say something about the prior probabilities of the competing hypotheses. Assignments of prior probabilities are often hard to justify, and they are *very* hard to justify in the present case. As noted in the previous section, there is no great difficulty in deciding what Susan's prior probability of having tuberculosis is. If all you know about her is that she comes from Wisconsin, it is reasonable to use the frequency of tuberculosis in Wisconsin as your estimate. Assigning prior probabilities to "big" scientific theories, like Einstein's general theory of relativity or Darwin's theory of evolution, is a different kettle of fish, and the same is true of "God exists." I argued in §2.10 that you shouldn't solve this problem by appealing to the principle of indifference. So what's a friend of the Bayesian design argument to do?

Swinburne (2004) claims that the God hypothesis is simple and that simpler theories have higher prior probabilities. This idea about the link between simplicity and prior probability has a history, one that has nothing special to do with design arguments. That history is not a happy one (Sober 2015).[40] The postulate that simpler theories should be assigned higher prior probabilities has been defended by saying that scientists can't consider all possible

---

[38] True, the surfaces of roses and fire engines both reflect red light and absorb other wavelengths, but that isn't a common cause, if cause must precede effect.

[39] Common cause explanations of a "matching" between two observed events often have higher likelihoods than their separate cause rivals; see Sober (2015, pp. 102–119) for a sufficient condition, and for examples in which violating that sufficient condition results in the separate cause explanation's being more likely.

[40] There is a special case in which simpler theories *clearly* have higher prior probabilities than theories that are more complex. For any propositions X and Y, $\Pr(X) \geq \Pr(X\&Y)$, and the inequality is strict if $\Pr(Y\ |\ X) < 1$. Here is a case in which simplicity goes with high probability. Unfortunately, this point does not extend to hypotheses that are incompatible with each other.

hypotheses at once, and that they therefore need to decide which hypotheses to consider first and which to consider only after earlier candidates have been refuted. This suggestion runs afoul of the fact that there are other ways to order hypotheses, and even if you do use the simplicity ordering to organize inquiry, that provides no reason to think that simpler theories have higher probabilities.

Swinburne (1997) gives a different argument for simplicity's epistemic relevance. He begins with the assumption that scientists and ordinary people are justified in believing a host of empirical propositions. He then argues that if simplicity were not a guide to truth, scientists and ordinary people would not be justified in holding those beliefs. His case for this conditional is that for each hypothesis we accept, there is another far more complex hypothesis that fits our observations equally well and contradicts what we accept. Swinburne concludes that simplicity is a guide to truth.

Swinburne's picture is that there is a single principle of simplicity that applies to inference problems in ordinary life, in science, and in philosophy. My picture is more fragmentary (Sober 2015); I think there are several such principles, and they need to be considered separately. Furthermore, I don't have much time for the idea that simplicity is rock bottom; when it is justified, it is justified because it reflects some deeper epistemic value (e.g., likelihood). It turns out that arguments that appeal to simplicity almost always depend on contingent assumptions about the problem at hand, and so such arguments need to be assessed on a case-by-case basis.

Even if simpler theories have higher prior probabilities, the question remains of how simple the God hypothesis is. It is sometimes claimed that God is a simple being in the sense of having no parts. However, this does not address the question of why theism is simpler than atheism. And if the God hypothesis says that numerous observed facts are the result of separate choices on God's part, it is extremely complex (Sober 2008).

3.5 Likelihoodist

Let's leave prior probabilities behind and move to a likelihoodist formulation of the design argument (§2.8):

Object o has characteristic C.
Pr(o has C | o was created by God) >
Pr(o has C | o was caused to exist by mindless process M).
The Law of Likelihood: observation X favors hypothesis H_1 over hypothesis H_2 if and only if Pr(X | H_1) > Pr(X | H_2).

The fact that o has C favors the God hypothesis over the hypothesis of mindless process M.

Notice how the law of likelihood parts ways with significance testing. According to the law, the assessment of evidence is essentially *contrastive*; it is the competition between *two* (or more) hypotheses that the evidence addresses.[41] The design hypothesis can't sit silently on the sidelines; *both* hypotheses need to say something about the probability of the observations. Point values aren't needed, of course, but the hypotheses must be sufficiently contentful that they tell you whether the observation is more probable under one hypothesis than it is under the other.

In this likelihood argument, I have taken care to formulate the hypothesis of intelligent design and its contrasting alternative so as not to trivialize the problem. If you observe that object o has characteristic C, and your two hypotheses are "God caused o to have C" and "mindless process M caused o to have C," each hypothesis entails the observation, so their likelihoods are both equal to one. This does not preclude your finding a difference in the prior probabilities of the two hypotheses, but changing the subject to these priors is to walk away from the idea that the observation provides discriminating evidence. For an observation to do so, you can't "pack" the observation into the competing hypotheses. You could, of course, pack the observation into one hypothesis but not the other, with the result that your pet hypothesis wins the likelihood competition. But that is a game that two can play, and it gets you nowhere.

John Arbuthnot (1710) consulted London christening records and saw that more boys than girls were born in each of the eighty years he surveyed. He further observed that boys die more frequently than girls as they grow up, with the result that the sex ratio is even at the time of marriage. Arbuthnot concluded that these observations favor the hypothesis that the sex ratio was created by God (who wanted every man to have a wife and every woman to have a husband) over the hypothesis of mindless chance, which says that each birth has a probability of $\frac{1}{2}$ of being a boy and $\frac{1}{2}$ of being a girl. I view Arbuthnot's argument through the lens of the law of likelihood (Sober 2011a), though others have interpreted him as performing the world's first significance test.

Arbuthnot's argument and its reception illustrate an important feature of likelihood arguments. Arbuthnot pitted the God hypothesis against a specific alternative, but did not consider others. His contemporary Nicolas Bernoulli agreed that the data favor God over Arbuthnot's chance hypothesis, but noted that God isn't more likely than a chance hypothesis that says that the

---

[41] It is misleading to formulate the law of likelihood as the claim that O supports H_1 better than O supports H_2 precisely when $\Pr(O \mid H_1) > \Pr(O \mid H_2)$. The law doesn't say that there is a noncontrastive notion of support.

probability of a male birth is $\frac{18}{35}$. When H_1 has a higher likelihood than H_2, given observation O, this leaves open whether H_1 also has a higher likelihood than H_3, again given O. Likelihood arguments are inevitably piecemeal. Rarely if ever can you survey all possible explanations of a given observation. The best you can do is assess the hypotheses at hand. Some see the contrastive character of likelihood thinking as an unsatisfactory limitation. I regard it as a fact of life.

The famous design argument about a watch and an eye, frequently credited to Paley (but see footnote 7), is often described as an argument from analogy, but it can easily be placed in a likelihood framework. The argument begins with the observation that the watch (w) is complex, functional, and delicate (*CFD*), and claims that this observation favors intelligent design over mindless chance:

Pr(w is *CFD* | w was made by an intelligent designer) >
Pr(w is *CFD* | w was made by a mindless chance process).

The fact that this inequality is true suggests that another is too. The eye (e) is observed to have the same triplet of features, and this observation of the eye has the same evidential significance as the observation of the watch:

Pr(e is *CFD* | e was made by an intelligent designer) >
Pr(e is *CFD* | e was made by a mindless chance process).

It does not matter to this likelihood argument how overall similar watches and eyes are; the likelihood argument is not an analogy argument (Sober 1990, 1993). I examine this likelihood argument in more detail in §4.

The fine-tuning argument also fits comfortably into a likelihood format (Sober 2003). That argument, you'll recall, begins with the idea that life would not be possible in our universe if the values of the constants that figure in physical laws differed more than a little from their actual values. The observation that the values of the physical constants fall in this narrow window is then said to favor the hypothesis that God set the values of those constants over the hypothesis that a mindless chance process did so. According to the law of likelihood, this thesis about favoring means that

Pr(the value of physical constant x is in W | God set the values of x & W is narrow) >
Pr(the value of physical constant x is in W | a mindless chance process set the value of x & W is narrow).

For simplicity, I'm focusing here on a single physical constant. W is the window that includes all and only the values of constant x that permit life to exist.

In this argument, God is assumed to be a life-loving deity, which means that the left-hand likelihood is big. The hypothesis of mindless chance described on the right-hand side seems to have a very small likelihood; after all, if the window is narrow and the range of logically possible values is wide, a mindless chance process has a very small probability of throwing the beanbag through the window. The fine-tuning argument therefore *seems* to be beyond reproach. However, there are reproaches to consider, which I do in Section 5.

I've been talking about "chance hypotheses," but what does that phrase encompass? Arbuthnot took "chance" to mean that each birth has a probability of $\frac{1}{2}$ of being a boy and $\frac{1}{2}$ of being a girl, but Bernouilli considered the hypothesis that the probabilities are $\frac{18}{35}$ and $\frac{17}{35}$. If Arbuthnot's is a chance hypothesis, is Bernouilli's also? Perhaps the chanciest chance hypothesis postulates a *flat probability distribution*, meaning that it says that all possible outcomes are equiprobable (more on this in Section 5); as a hypothesis departs from flatness, calling the hypothesis by that moniker becomes less and less natural. Arbuthnot's and Bernouilli's hypotheses are both pretty chancy.

We sometimes talk about outcomes being "due to chance." This often means that they are very improbable. According to Arbuthnot's $p = \frac{1}{2}$ hypothesis, the male-biased sex ratio observed over each of eighty years was "due to chance," but this result was to be expected according to Bernouilli's $p = \frac{18}{35}$. Fisher (1930) remarked that it is not a matter of chance when a casino turns a profit each year, since that outcome is overwhelmingly probable. The outcome of each gamble is a matter of chance, but the positive bottom line at year's end is anything but. Fisher also denied that the evolution of adaptive traits in the process of natural selection is a matter of chance. The point about "try and try again" from §2.2 is pertinent here.

3.6 Abductive

Abduction (C. S. Peirce's term, now often used as a synonym for *inference to the best explanation*) provides yet another framework for formulating design arguments:

We observe that object *o* has characteristic *C*.

If an intelligent designer made *o*, that would explain why *o* has *C*, and that explanation would be better than the alternative explanations.

—————————————————

Therefore, probably an intelligent designer made *o*.

Abduction is little more than a label until a theory is offered about what makes one hypothesis a better explanation than another. One approach is Bayesian; you equate "*X* is a better explanation than *Y* of *E*" with "*X* has a higher posterior probability than *Y*, given *E*." This approach makes the word "explanation" misleading; inference to the best explanation should just be called "inference to the most probable hypothesis" (Lipton 2004).

A second strategy is to list the "explanatory virtues" a hypothesis might have, such as fitting the observations, consistency with background knowledge, generality, precision, simplicity, coherence, unification, and fruitfulness (Lipton 2004; Psillos 2007), with no commitment to this list's having a Bayesian rationale. Now two challenges arise. The first concerns *weighting* – which of two explanations is better overall, if each has virtues that the other lacks? The second concerns whether the alternative explanations considered must be exhaustive, or can just be the ones that have already been formulated. If the former, you'll be hard-pressed to show that what you have before you really is the best; if the latter, it isn't clear why the best explanation you have at hand isn't just "the best of a bad lot" (van Fraassen 1989) and so should not be thought probable.[42]

These reservations seem not to apply to a design argument that seeks to explain why the fundamental scientific laws that govern our universe are true. A fundamental law is standardly defined as a law that can't be explained by any other law. I take this to mean that if there are fundamental laws, then they can't be explained by anything that science will ever be able to access. A God hypothesis then steps up to the plate. That hypothesis is claimed to be the best explanation for why the fundamental laws are true for the simple reason that it is the only conceivable explanation (Swinburne 1968, p. 204).

One response to this abductive argument begins with the possibility that fundamental laws might be brute facts, meaning that they have no explanation at all. The abductive design argument we're considering sweeps past this possibility, but why? Ignoring it can't be justified by insisting that every proposition has an explanation (or that all contingent propositions do). Nor can it be finessed by asserting that inference to the best explanation has good scientific credentials and that science is therefore obliged to sanction any explanation that is the only game in town. The hypothesis that God did it, if true, would explain why fundamental law *F* is true. The hypothesis that *F* is a brute fact, if true, would not explain why *F* is true. Inference to the best

---

[42] Likelihood arguments aren't subject to this objection, since they don't aim to determine which hypothesis is more probable than not.

explanation takes this difference to be decisive, but it is far from clear that it is (Priest 1981).

Swinburne (2004) argues that if you believe that God explains why the fundamental laws are true, then there will be just one unexplained explainer in your corpus of beliefs. Without this belief, there will be more (if there is more than one fundamental law). Theism is therefore simpler in the sense that it has fewer unexplained postulates. It does not follow, however, that theism has a higher posterior probability than atheism, which is what the abductive argument for theism asserts.

3.7 Concluding Comments

In this section, I have concentrated on evaluating the strengths and weaknesses of various forms of argument, not on identifying what specific design theorists intended to say. The latter topic often leads to controversy. For example, Oppy (2002) and Jantzen (2014) both classify Paley's design argument as deductive (though the premises they identify are related to each other inductively); Schupbach (2005) says the argument is an inference to the best explanation. All these versions of Paley's argument encounter problems, or so I have suggested. I do not claim that Paley had the law of likelihood in mind.

It is possible that the flawed argument forms I have described in this section can be retooled.[43] If so, my criticisms stand as a warning against oversimple conceptions of analogy, induction, inference to the best explanation, and so on.

The main conclusion of this section is that the strongest design arguments are likelihood inferences. The strength of this form of inference derives in part from its circumspection. You are not trying to prove that God must exist, or that God probably exists, nor are you attempting to compare the God hypothesis with all possible alternative hypotheses. Rather, a likelihood formulation of a design argument draws the modest conclusion that a given observation is evidence favoring the God hypothesis over this or that specific alternative hypothesis.[44] In the next two sections, I argue that even this modest goal is not so easily achieved.

It may seem that likelihood arguments are useless because they don't indicate which hypotheses you should believe. This reaction, I suspect, confuses pointlessness with insufficiency. Design arguments, in all their guises, are supposed to be empirical. This doesn't mean that the premises idly cite

---

[43] For a critical review of theories of analogical reasoning, see Bartha (2016).

[44] I have no objection to calling this likelihood inference an inference to the *better* explanation, except that friends of abduction usually think there are factors additional to likelihood that affect a hypothesis's explanatory goodness, and they usually want abductive arguments to conclude that the best explanation is probably true.

observations; it means that those observations have to do real work. If the observations cited do not favor intelligent design over alternatives, they cannot justify belief in the design hypothesis.

4 Biological Creationism

4.1 No Packing In!

I suggested in Section 3 that design arguments are strongest when they have a likelihood format. If a design argument claims that object o's having characteristic C is evidence favoring the God hypothesis over the hypothesis that mindless process M was at work, a good way to interpret this is the following:

(API)   Pr(o has C | God decided whether o would have C) >
       Pr(o has C | mindless process M settled whether o would have C).[45]

Notice that I did *not* formulate the likelihood claim like this:

Pr(o has C | God caused o to have C) >
Pr(o has C | mindless process M caused o to have C).

This second inequality is false, since both probabilities have values of one. Remember the warning in §3.5 about "packing" observations into hypotheses. The API formulation *avoids packing in*.

API contrasts two specific hypotheses – one postulates God's intentional action, the other a specific mindless process M. API does not contrast the God hypothesis with the catchall hypothesis that some mindless process or other was responsible. This choice reflects likelihoodism's aversion to catchall hypotheses (§2.10). Since creationism's main stalking horse since 1859 has been Darwin's theory, I focus in this section on natural selection as the specific mindless process of interest.

Intelligent design proponents often are content to consider catchall hypotheses. For example, Michael Behe (2006) writes:

> If one simply contrasts intelligent causes with unintelligent causes, as ID does, then those two categories do constitute a mutually exclusive and exhaustive set of possible explanations. Thus evidence against the ability of unintelligent causes to explain a phenomenon does strengthen the case for an intelligent cause.

---

[45] In API, the God hypothesis entails that o exists. The hypothesis is therefore falsifiable (Sober 2007b). However, the existence of o does not discriminate between God and mindless process M.

Behe is talking about *two* catchalls, not just *one*. There are many possible intelligent designers, and there are many possible mindless processes. I think that comparing the likelihoods of these two catchalls is a hopeless undertaking. This does not phase Behe, however, since he thinks the design argument is inductive, not likelihoodist (see footnote 37). I explained in §3.2 why I think the inductive formulation is flawed.

4.2 Extending Duhem's Thesis

The historian and philosopher of science Pierre Duhem (1914) made an important point about theories in physics. His claim was that physical theories, on their own, do not make observational predictions; rather, theories are able to do this only when supplemented with auxiliary assumptions. Duhem's thesis, as it now is called, can be schematized as follows:

$T \not\rightarrow O$, but $T\&A \rightarrow O$

The arrow represents the relation of deductive entailment. It is easy to see why this thesis is true for a theory like Newtonian mechanics (the laws of motion plus the law of universal gravitation). That theory leaves open whether there is any matter in the universe. It just says that *if* there is matter with this-or-that configuration, then thus-and-so will ensue. Notice the *if*! To get the theory to make a prediction about what you'll now observe, you need to make assumptions about the existence of objects and their properties.

Duhem's thesis can be extended to theories and observations that are related nondeductively: *it is often true that theories confer probabilities on observational claims only when those theories are supplemented with auxiliary assumptions* (Sober 1999, 2003). We often can't assign a value to $\Pr(O \mid T)$, but we can do so for $\Pr(O \mid T\&A)$.[46]

Here's a mundane example. You are a cook in a restaurant and the waiter enters the kitchen from the dining room and tells you that someone ordered oatmeal for breakfast. You wonder whether the customer was your friend Jane or your friend Joe. This leads you to consider whether the order favors the Jane hypothesis over the Joe in the now-familiar sense that

Pr(the order is for oatmeal | Jane placed the order) >
Pr(the order is for oatmeal | Joe placed the order).

If you have no idea what Jane and Joe tend to eat, you will be unable to say whether this inequality is true.

---

[46] This means that my brief discussion in §2.10 of Eddington's data favoring Einstein's theory over Newton's was simplified, since it failed to make explicit the role of auxiliary assumptions.

4.3 How *Not* to Obtain the Needed Auxiliary Assumptions

Since auxiliary assumptions are needed to test the Jane hypothesis against the Joe, why not just invent the needed assumptions? For example, you could assume that Jane loves oatmeal and that Joe loathes it. That assumption is enough to get your observation to discriminate between the two hypotheses. The obvious problem is that this assumption is arbitrary. You could just as easily assume that it is Jane who loathes and Joe who loves, and you'd then conclude that the breakfast order favors Joe over Jane. Or you could assume that Jane and Joe have the same food proclivities, with the result that there is a likelihood equality.

I hope the prosaic character of this example doesn't lead you to think that it has nothing to do with science. In testing hypotheses against each other in science, auxiliary assumptions are needed, but it is no good just *inventing* them. They need to be justified. In particular, they need to be *independently* justified (Kitcher 1983; Sober 1999), but what does "independence" mean here?

Independence requires, first, that your justification for an auxiliary assumption about how Jane and Joe feel about oatmeal can't be that you believe that it was Jane who placed the order. Of course, if she *did* place the order, that would mean that she probably wanted oatmeal. However, your goal is to *test* the hypothesis that Jane placed the order, so you can't *assume* at the outset that this hypothesis is true. The general point is that if you want to test H_1 against H_2, the auxiliary assumptions you use can't depend for their justification on the assumption that H_1 is true or on the assumption that H_2 is. You may have an opinion about who placed the breakfast order, but you need to set that opinion aside if you want to assess the likelihoods of the competing hypotheses.

The second requirement is more surprising. If you want to see whether observation O favors H_1 over H_2, your auxiliaries can't depend for their justification on the assumption that O is true. The reason for this is that if you assume that O is true, you can deduce that "*notH$_1$* or O" and "*notH$_2$* or O" are both true. These disjunctive auxiliary assumptions lead to a likelihood equality:

$$Pr[O \mid H_1 \ \& \ (notH_1 \ or \ O)] = Pr[O \mid H_2 \ \& \ (notH_2 \ or \ O)] = 1.$$

Using O to construct auxiliary assumptions would have disastrous consequences for inquiry, both inside science and out. It would mean that observations never discriminate between competing hypotheses. Science would no longer be an empirical enterprise.

I've made two negative claims, each describing how auxiliary assumptions can fail to be independently justified, but what can be said in a positive vein? At least two pathways are available for independently justifying the auxiliary assumptions that allow you to determine whether observation O favors hypothesis H_1 over hypothesis H_2. First, you may have evidence that A is probably true that avoids the two pitfalls just mentioned. For example, maybe you earlier saw Jane and Joe consume multiple breakfasts; this may justify assumptions about what their food preferences probably are (Sober 2004). Second, even if you have no justified probabilities for auxiliary assumptions, you still may have observations (distinct from O) that strongly favor auxiliary A over known alternatives (in the sense of the law of likelihood). For example, astrophysicists who want to determine whether the current trajectory of an asteroid discriminates between two hypotheses about its earlier position can use general relativity as an auxiliary assumption. They are entitled to do so since other observations strongly favor relativity theory over Newtonian mechanics.

4.4 Likelihoods for God Hypotheses

My discussion of Duhem's thesis sets the stage for my objection to likelihood versions of biological design arguments. Suppose a design argument asserts that

Pr(vertebrates have eyes that have features F_1 | God gave organisms their features) > Pr(vertebrates have eyes that have features F_1 | mindless natural selection caused organisms to have their features).

The problem I have with this claim is that there is no saying whether the first of these probabilities is big, middling, or small. Sure, you can invent auxiliary assumptions that settle this; the problem is that there is no way to independently ascertain whether God would want to give eyes to vertebrates, whether God would want to give all vertebrates the same kind of eye, and whether God would want those eyes to have features F_1 rather than F_2, or F_3, . . ., or F_n (Venn 1866, pp. 254–260; Salmon 1978, p. 157; Sober 2003). This problem remains in place even if there is a justification for thinking that God is all-powerful, all-knowing, and all-good (all-PKG, for short).

This point about the God hypothesis, if correct, is fatal to likelihood versions of the biological design argument, regardless of whether evolutionary theory is able to say how probable it is that vertebrates have eyes that have features F_1. Later in this section, I argue that evolutionary hypotheses can often be tested against each other by comparing their likelihoods, but that is icing on the cake.

4.5 Step by Step Versus All at Once

Biologists think the evolution of complex adaptive structures is a stepwise process. The vertebrate eye didn't evolve all at once in an ancestral population that had no eyes; rather, there was an evolving lineage in which simple eyes first evolved, after which more complex eyes gradually emerged. This is the gradualism that Darwin embraced and that continues to be a guiding idea in modern biology. It is not a dogma, but has considerable observational support, as I explain later.

What do creationists say about God's process of creation? Did God start with the idea that there would be vertebrates, and then decide to give them camera eyes? Or did God start with the idea that there would be camera eyes, and then decide that there should be vertebrates that house those eyes? Or did God create plans instantaneously, without this sort of stepwise reasoning? Creationists cannot answer these questions without leaving natural theology behind.

The evolutionary changes that can occur in a lineage are constrained by the characteristics that ancestors have. The reason modern zebras don't have machine guns with which to repel lion attacks is not that those devices would have been useless. The reason is that the mutations needed for that device to evolve were not present in ancestors. Natural selection can work only on the available variation (Krebs and Davies 1981).

God suffers from no such limitation. If God is omniscient, God knows what all possible organisms would be like. If God is omnipotent, God has the power to create any of those possibilities. It is unfathomable why a God like this would actualize the organisms we now observe rather than other possibilities (assuming, still, the strictures of natural theology). In contrast, it is unsurprising that present organisms have the features they do, given the characteristics of their ancestors, if known evolutionary processes caused changes in lineages. The gradualism of adaptive evolution allows evolutionary biology to address problems that creationism cannot solve.

4.6 Forward Sampling to the Rescue?

In §3.2, I discussed an inductive sampling version of the design argument. The idea was to estimate the value of Pr(an intelligent designer made object o | o has characteristic C) by looking at objects that have C and tracing their causal histories back in time to observe how often we see them stem from an intelligent designer. I called this a *backward induction*, since the inference runs from present to past. I criticized this argument, but maybe the sampling idea can solve the problem we now are considering about the designer's goals. Can we estimate the value of

(FI)   Pr(object o has characteristic C | an intelligent designer intentionally made o)

by looking at known intelligent designers and tracing them forward in time to see how often they intentionally make objects with characteristic *C* (McGrew 2004)? This is a *forward induction* (FI).

This sampling procedure allows you to estimate that the probability isn't zero when *C* is the trait of being complex, functional, and delicate (where delicacy, recall, means that the structure would not be able to function if one of its parts were modified or removed). Although human designers sometimes make such objects, the estimated probability isn't very big. Many of the things that human designers make don't perform their functions. Of those that do perform a function, many are simple. And of the complex functional objects that human designers are observed to make, many of them aren't delicate. Human designers often like to make devices that exhibit *redundancy*; these devices perform their functions even when parts are modified or removed. That's why buildings usually don't fall down when a single brick is removed.[47] And don't forget that nonhuman organisms sometimes make and use tools. They arguably are intelligent designers, so their productions may need to be figured into the FI estimate.

Although the estimated value of the FI probability is nonzero when *C* is the characteristic of being complex, functional, and delicate, matters change if we turn to the trait of being alive. We have never seen an intelligent designer make a living thing by first designing it and then (successfully) carrying out the plan, so our sample leads to an estimate of zero for the value of FI in this case.[48]

There is another problem. Why should an estimate of the FI probability be of any use with respect to the design argument, which is about the existence of God, not about the existence of some unspecified intelligent designer? God is very different from us humans. The fact that humans often make cooking utensils doesn't mean that God has a good probability of doing the same. This point is specific to extrapolations from the goals of human beings to God's; it does not entail a wholesale inductive skepticism.

4.7 An Objection to My Objection

I've criticized the biological design argument for assuming that we know enough about God's goals to say, even approximately, what the likelihood is of the God hypothesis, given the observed features of organisms. It might be objected that we often are able to tell that an intelligent designer made an object

---

[47] Nature often follows suit, which is why many organisms have *two* kidneys, *two* lungs, and so on (Shanks and Joplin 1999).

[48] Artificial selection is not a counterexample to this claim. Plant and animal breeders work with populations of organisms and modify their trait frequencies; they don't build organisms from nonliving materials (at least not yet).

even though we have no idea what that putative designer's goals were. I once discussed a putative example of this sort – the experience that the biologist John Maynard Smith had during World War II when he inspected warehouses full of captured German materiel (Sober 2003). Maynard Smith couldn't tell what these machines were for, but they obviously were made by intelligent designers. He knew *that* intelligent designers made them without knowing in any detail *why* the designers made them.

My reply was and is that Maynard Smith was assuming that the putative designers he was thinking about had goals much like those that he knew from his prior experience with people. An object with dials and knobs and wires is not terribly improbable, if a twentieth-century *human* engineer was the designer in question. Maynard Smith knew that his contemporaries often *wanted* to build devices with these features. Seeing this doesn't require a deeper understanding of what a machine is for.

I am not saying that you can attribute intelligent design only if you think that the designer in question is human. If you detect a radio signal of a certain type from a distant galaxy, you perhaps will reason that the hypothesis of intelligent design is more probable than the hypothesis of mindless chance, and you will not be deterred by your strong conviction that no human beings are there. This was the point that Cleanthes made about the voice from the sky; modern friends of the design argument make the same point by imagining us finding something just like a human artifact adrift in a far reach of the universe (see, e.g., McGrew 2004). However, the present section is about *likelihood* formulations of biological design arguments. The suggestion that you can tell that an object was probably made by an intelligent designer, given the object's observed features, is a claim about the *probabilities* of hypotheses, not their *likelihoods*. I discussed this very different type of argument in §3.2 under the heading of inductive sampling, and criticized it. It's the likelihood formulation that requires assumptions about the putative designer's goals.

4.8 For the Good of What?

When creationists cite adaptive traits as evidence for God's handiwork, they usually assume that God is benevolent. Here I want to focus on the question of which biological entities are the objects of that benevolence. Does God want *organisms* to do well, or *groups* of organisms to do well, or the *genes* within organisms to do well? If these three levels of organization were all in the same boat, the choice wouldn't matter. If what is good for genes is to build well-functioning organisms, and what is good for organisms is to build well-functioning groups, this question for creationists would not be pressing.

This easy solution is not available, however, since nature is peppered with characteristics that are good for objects at one level of organization but bad for objects at another. Honeybees have barbed stingers. When a bee stings an intruder to the hive, the bee eviscerates itself and dies, though the stinger, torn from the bee, remains in place and continues to pump venom. The barbed stinger isn't good for the individual honeybee, but it is good for the hive. There also are conflicts of interest between *genes* and the organisms in which those genes are found. There is a gene in the house mouse called the *t*-allele that enhances its representation in the next generation by subverting the ability of other genes in the same organism to do so. The *t*-allele does a fine job of taking care of itself, but it causes males that have two copies of the gene to be sterile.[49] Another example is closer to home. Cancer cells replicate faster than normal cells in the same organism. Cancer resembles the *t*-allele. Both are examples of *intragenomic conflict*, wherein the genes inside a single organism compete with each other; this phenomenon was unknown to Darwin, but now is an important subject in evolutionary biology.

Apparently, if God built the living world, God had different goals in different projects. Sometimes God wanted organisms to have traits that help them to survive and reproduce, but at other times God wanted groups to have traits that help them to avoid extinction and to found daughter groups, and made this possible by giving organisms traits that reduce their ability to survive and reproduce. At still other times, God wanted to promote some genes at the expense of others, even when those favored genes aren't good for the organisms that house them. This shifting picture of God's goals can of course be invented piecemeal to fit your observations, but that isn't cricket. As I have emphasized, you need an *independently* justified picture of what God's goals would be if God existed.

These mysteries about God's benevolence disappear when you ask the question of what natural selection "cares" about. Of course, natural selection is a mindless process, so this "caring" is metaphorical. My question concerns the types of traits that selection will cause to increase in frequency. Will it favor traits that help organisms, or groups of organisms, or parts of organisms (like genes)? The helping involved must in each case consist in benefits to an object's survival and reproduction.

Darwin thought about the honeybee's stinger in the same way he thought about sterile workers in the social insects. These and other examples motivated

---

[49] The *t*-allele distorts the process of "fair" meiosis. Heterozygotes normally form sex cells (sperms and eggs) so that 50% of the cells have genes from one chromosome and 50% have genes from the other. This isn't what happens to heterozygotes that have one copy of the *t*-allele and one copy of an alternative allele. Their sex cells are about 85% *t* (Crow 1979).

him to expand his picture of natural selection. Tigers now have sharp teeth because organisms in the lineage with sharp teeth did better in the struggle for existence than organisms with dull teeth. This is *individual selection*, wherein individuals in the same group of conspecifics compete with each other. Darwin added to this the idea of *group selection* – that groups sometimes compete with each other (Sober 2011). Hives that have bees with barbed stingers do better than hives that have bees with barbless stingers. Biologists now use the term "altruistic" to label traits that are good for the group but bad for the individual, and "selfish" to label traits that have the opposite upshot. The problem of how altruistic characteristics can evolve has been an important topic in evolutionary biology. Although prominent biologists attacked the concept of group selection in the 1960s, it now is part of the conceptual toolkit that biologists widely view as legitimate (Sober and Wilson 1998).

The view of natural selection I've just described is called *multilevel selection theory*. It says that natural selection causes different traits to evolve because they benefit objects at different levels of organization.[50] Some traits evolve because they enhance an organism's fitness (its prospects for survival and reproduction); others evolve because they help groups to avoid extinction and to found daughter colonies; and still others evolve because they help genes to outcompete other genes in the same organism.[51] Given this pluralistic view, how is one to tell what sorts of traits will evolve? The key is to look at the pattern of variation in fitness that competing traits have. Consider an altruistic trait. If it is found in just one population, along with a selfish trait, the altruistic trait will probably decline in frequency and selfishness will sweep to fixation. However, if the trait is represented in several groups in the same species, and the groups differ in their frequencies of altruism, then individual and group selection will both occur. In this two-level process, selfishness beats altruism within groups, but altruistic groups do better than selfish groups. The question is which of these opposing forces is stronger; the answer will tell you whether altruism will probably evolve.

The pattern of variation in fitness, both within and between groups, is often observable. Here's an example that David Wilson and I used to introduce the subject of group selection in our book *Unto Others*:

---

[50] I here give short shrift to the selfish gene picture that Dawkins (1976) popularized – that selection favors a trait precisely when that trait helps genes to increase in frequency. This view is either trivial or false. It is trivial if it is compatible with genes evolving because they are good for the groups in which they occur. It is false if it denies that. For longer shrifts, see Sober (1984) and Sober and Wilson (1998).

[51] Indeed, it is left open that a single trait might help objects at different levels; for example, a trait might evolve because it benefits the organisms that have the trait and also because it benefits the groups in which it occurs.

> There is a parasite that migrates from snails to ants to the livers of cows and sheep, and then loops back again. A group of these parasites spends two generations in a snail after which the parasites enclose themselves in a mucus mass ... which exits the snail and is eaten by ants. An ant eats about 50 of these packages in a meal. The parasites then bore through the ant's stomach, and one of them migrates to the ant's brain where it forms a thin-walled cyst, known as the brain worm. The other parasites in the ant form thick-walled cysts. The brain worm changes the behavior of the ant, causing it to spend a lot of time at the tips of grass blades, which makes the ant more prone to be eaten by livestock, in whose bodies the parasite continues its life cycle. (Sober and Wilson 1998, p. 18)

The brain worm is altruistic; it sacrifices its life and thereby helps the other parasites in the same ant to move from that host to livestock. In this example as in so many others, the workings of natural selection are not shrouded in mystery. In contrast, there are no clear answers when one asks for details concerning what God's benevolence really means for the features that genes, organisms, and groups might exhibit.[52]

4.9 Neutral and Deleterious Traits

Evolutionary biologists who criticize the design argument often focus on traits of organisms that are neutral or deleterious. In doing so, they are following in Darwin's (1859, p. 402) footsteps:

> On the view of each organism with all its separate parts having been specially created, how utterly inexplicable is it that organs bearing the plain stamp of inutility ... should so frequently occur.

Darwin (1859, p. 420) adds that useless organs are no surprise according to his theory:

> On the view of descent with modification, we may conclude that the existence of organs in a rudimentary, imperfect, and useless condition, or quite aborted, far from presenting a strange difficulty, as they assuredly do on the old doctrine of creation, might even have been anticipated in accordance with the views here explained.

Darwin's wording suggests that he is offering an inference to the best explanation (§3.6). What happens to his remarks if they are placed in a likelihood framework?

When Darwin says that neutral and deleterious organs (the two types of inutility) are "inexplicable" according to the God hypothesis, does he mean that they have a low probability according to that hypothesis, or that we don't know

---

[52] For a detailed introduction to philosophical discussion of units of selection, see Lloyd (2017).

what probability they have? If the latter, Darwin is endorsing the criticism of the design argument that I have stated. However, Darwin sometimes seems to assume that God would not want organisms, especially human beings, to have deleterious traits, and so such traits should not exist if the God hypothesis were true. Many of Darwin's successors have argued along the same lines (e.g., Gould 1980).

This Darwinian argument against intelligent design is flawed. If a trait's being neutral or deleterious favors evolutionary theory over the God hypothesis, then a trait's being advantageous must have the opposite evidential significance. As noted in §2.8, the law of likelihood entails a symmetry:

$$\Pr(O \mid H_1) > \Pr(O \mid H_2) \text{ if and only if } \Pr(notO \mid H_2) > \Pr(notO \mid H_1).$$

However, few evolutionists would want to concede that a trait's being advantageous favors the God hypothesis over the hypothesis of mindless evolution, and they are right to resist that conclusion. Theists sometimes think that a trait's being advantageous is evidence *for* God's handiwork; atheists sometimes think that a trait's being disadvantageous is evidence *against*. The conclusions are opposite, but the mistake is the same.

Some creationists agree with my claim that we can't discern God's goals with enough precision to tell whether the God hypothesis says that the observed traits of organisms have high probability or low. For example, Phillip Johnson (1991), in his book *Darwin on Trial*, says that God's purposes are "inscrutable" (p. 67) and "mysterious" (p. 71). Michael Behe comes to a similar conclusion when he criticizes the claim that imperfect adaptations refute the design hypothesis. Behe (1996, p. 223) says that the problem with

> ... the argument from imperfection is that it critically depends on psycho-analysis of the unidentified designer. Yet the reasons that a designer would or would not do anything are virtually impossible to know unless the designer tells you specifically what those reasons are.

As mentioned in Section 1, Behe prefers to talk about an unidentified designer rather than God, but his point applies to the latter just as much as it applies to the former. We can't say that imperfect adaptations refute intelligent design, Behe claims, because that requires us to know the designer's intentions, and this is something we cannot do. Behe thinks this lack of knowledge does no harm to the design argument, since he takes that argument to be inductive (§3.2). However, Behe's point is devastating if the design argument is about likelihoods.

Behe's colleagues in the intelligent design movement have not always followed his advice to avoid psychoanalysis. In the 1970s and 1980s, several biologists conjectured that the genomes of many species contain lots of "junk DNA," meaning genetic material that makes no positive contribution to the survival and reproduction of organisms. Junk DNA was sometimes thought to be strictly neutral with respect to the fitness of organisms, but it was often recognized that organisms pay a metabolic cost for their DNA; this means that junk DNA is slightly deleterious (but not so deleterious that selection on organisms would summarily eliminate it). The idea of junk DNA was attractive in biology, and remains so, in part because there is no correlation between organismic complexity and genome size. For example, onion genomes are five times as big as human genomes and lungfish genomes are thirty-six times as large (Palazzo and Gregory 2014).

Multilevel selection theory makes room for the idea that some DNA exists for reasons having nothing to do with helping organisms to survive and reproduce. If some stretches of DNA make copies of themselves and spread those copies within an individual's genome, whereas alternative configurations do not do so, and both are neutral (or only mildly deleterious) with respect to organismic fitness, the better spreaders will win the within-organism competition (Doolittle and Sapienza 1980; Orgel and Crick 1980).

After the junk DNA hypothesis was proposed, functions were discovered for pieces of the genome (e.g., some introns) that some biologists earlier had claimed to have no organismic function. Dembski (1998b), Meyer (2009), Wells (2011), and others in the ID camp saw this as a victory for intelligent design theory and a defeat for evolutionary theory. There are two flaws in their triumphant story. Evolutionary theory does say that organisms may have features that are useless or deleterious to them. But the theory, properly construed, isn't committed to the thesis that all introns are functionless. The conjecture that an intron lacks organismic function is a conjecture, similar to the earlier claim that the human appendix has no organismic function. That claim turned out to be wrong – the appendix houses useful gut flora – but that doesn't show that the theory of evolution is wrong. The same goes for introns and their ilk. It is important to distinguish the *theory* of evolution from the conjectures that this or that evolutionary *theorist* floats. Refuting the latter doesn't necessarily refute the former.

The other mistake is the claim that intelligent design theory "predicted" that junk DNA is rare or nonexistent. True, some intelligent design *theorists* made this prediction, but what is the *theory* from which they drew? Is their theory the thesis that an intelligent designer of organisms would never allow organisms to have traits that are neutral or deleterious? Presumably not, since that commitment would allow any such trait to refute the ID hypothesis. Cancer and the *t*-allele would suffice. It is important to distinguish the claims advanced by this or that intelligent design theorist from the "theory" of intelligent design. Of course the *theorists* exist and they sometimes make predictions, but *there is no there there* when it comes to a predictive *theory* (Sarkar 2007).[53]

4.10 The Problem of Evil

In its strong form, the argument from evil tries to deduce the nonexistence of God from the fact that there is so much evil in the world.[54] The argument is often formulated with the assumption that God, if there is such a being, is all-powerful, all-knowing, and perfectly good (all-PKG). Theists often see no way to explain why an all-PKG being would allow so much evil to exist, but they often also feel that this puzzle doesn't oblige them to abandon their belief. They point out that it is very hard for human beings to understand what God's goals are. I agree that this is difficult, but I find it odd that theists who have this reaction to the argument from evil should be moved even a little by the biological design argument. If God's goals are opaque when it comes to the problem of evil, why aren't they also opaque when it comes to the characteristics of organisms?

In Section 1, I provisionally defined "God" as a being who intentionally created the universe. This definition leaves open whether God is all-PKG. In consequence, the existence of imperfect adaptations, of neutral and deleterious traits, and of evils aplenty all fail to prove that God does not exist.

The all-PKG conception of God is an auxiliary assumption in the Duhemian sense defined some pages back. It is an assumption that many atheists and theists embrace. But these commitments aside, why should this assumption about God's characteristics be accepted? Does the assumption have an independent justification?[55] True, it is part of some religion traditions, but it isn't part of others, and sacred texts and traditions have no place in *natural* theology. In addition, even if you *do* define God as all-PKG, the problem remains of discerning the goals God had in giving organisms some characteristics rather than others.

---

[53] This is not to deny that intelligent design proponents have lots to say about why evolutionary theory is flawed and lots to say about how intelligent design can be detected.

[54] There is a more modest version of the argument from evil, which is called the *evidential* argument from evil. Instead of trying to prove that God doesn't exist, the evidential argument tries to show that some of the evils we observe are evidence against God's existence. Draper (1989) gives this argument a likelihood formulation, as do I (Sober 2003, 2008, 2009, 2015).

[55] In Hume's *Dialogues* (11.15), Philo argues that the evidence favors the hypothesis that the cause or causes of order in the universe (this is the working definition of "God") have "neither goodness nor malice" – they are indifferent to both well-being and suffering.

4.11 Likelihoods for Evolutionary Hypotheses

If there are no independently justified auxiliary assumptions that permit the God hypothesis to confer probabilities on the characteristics we observe organisms to have, the likelihood formulation of the biological design argument is dead in the water. There is no need to examine what evolutionary theory says about the probabilities of those observations. However, doing so is instructive, since it highlights the fact that evolutionary theory is a substantive fruitful theory whereas intelligent design "theory" is nothing of the kind.

First, a general comment. When you ask what probability evolutionary theory assigns to some fact about current organisms (e.g., that vertebrates now have eyes with features F_1), you need to be clear about what the propositions are on which you are conditionalizing. Are you interested in the probability of the fact, given just the state of the universe at the time of the Big Bang (about 14 billion years ago), or the state of the Earth when it first came into existence (about 4.5 billion years ago), or the state of the Earth when life began (about 4 billion years ago), or the state of eukaryotes (organisms whose cells have nuclei) when they first appeared (about 2 billion years ago)? Additional options are available. Imagine a time line that stretches from the Big Bang to now. The probability of a present event can change as time marches on.

Evolutionary biologists rarely consider the probabilities of present events given the state of the universe many billions of years ago. Instead, they usually conditionalize on more recent events. The problems they address usually dictate the relevant temporal frames, as the following examples show. These examples often involve likelihood *comparisons*; it isn't the point value of a single likelihood that matters, but whether observations discriminate between competing evolutionary hypotheses.

The hypothesis of universal common ancestry – that all current life on Earth traces back to a single common ancestor – is defended by citing a variety of evidence. An example is the near universality of the genetic code. There are many possible genetic codes[56] that would work, but most groups of organisms use just one of them, while a few use codes that differ only a little from the common code. If an organism uses a code, there is strong selection for it to continue to do so. An organism that changes its code will probably be inviable. In addition, if the organism is sexual, it probably won't be able to produce viable fertile offspring if it changes its code from the one that is common in the species. This means that

---

[56] DNA and RNA are sequences of nucleotides. A genetic code is a set of rules that describe how sequences of nucleotide triplets, called *codons*, dictate which amino acids will be added during protein synthesis. Organisms differ in their nucleotide sequences, but they mostly follow the same code.

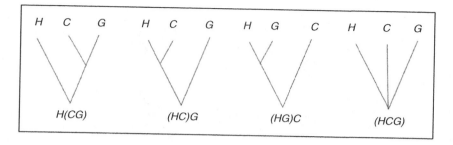

Figure 3 Four phylogenetic hypotheses about how humans (*H*), chimpanzees (*C*), and gorillas (*G*) are genealogically related

Pr(code *C* is almost universal | universal common ancestry) >
Pr(code *C* is almost universal | separate ancestry).

The separate ancestry hypothesis can take different forms. It can assert that all present organisms trace back to two and no fewer common ancestors, that they trace back to three and no fewer, and so on (Sober and Steel 2002). The argument for this likelihood inequality depends on the assumption that multiple genetic codes are workable (Sober and Steel 2017).[57]

Evolutionary biologists consider numerous more specific questions about genealogy. For example, if present-day humans, chimpanzees, and gorillas have a common ancestor, are two of them more closely related to each other than either is to the third? If so, which two? Figure 3 depicts four possible phylogenetic trees. To evaluate them, biologists gather morphological, physiological, and genetic data from the three groups of present organisms. Given the law of likelihood, the question is which of these four hypotheses makes the data most probable. As required by Duhem's thesis, biologists recognize that this question can be answered only if auxiliary assumptions are adopted concerning the kinds of evolutionary processes that are at work in the branches of these phylogenetic trees. For example, you might restrict your attention to traits that you think are selectively neutral and then use a process model that says that this is so. Where there is uncertainty about the process, several auxiliary assumptions can be considered.

To investigate whether and how natural selection affected the evolution of a trait currently found in a lineage, you usually need information about the other traits that were already present. This raises the question of how earlier states of

---

[57] The genetic code is an evolved characteristic, so it isn't a precondition for evolution to occur. Meyer (2009, pp. 274–275) erroneously asserts that evolution by natural selection requires that a genetic code is already present, from which he concludes that selection can't explain the existence of a code. What is true is that evolution by natural selection requires *parent/offspring correlation*; this correlation needn't be induced by genes.

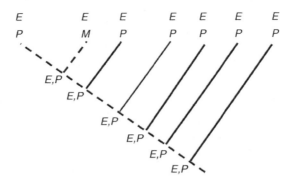

Figure 4 If an even sex ratio (*E*) is found in all tips of the tree, but monogamy
(*M*) is found in only the one shown, the others being polygynous (*P*), it is
reasonable to infer that the ancestors shown in the broken-line lineage had
E and *P*. If so, *M* evolved after *E* was already in place.

the lineage can be ascertained. Is the evolutionary past hidden from us, just as
God's goals are? The answer is *no*, thanks to the fact of common ancestry.
Possibly inspired by Arbuthnot's design argument about human sex ratio
(§3.5), which rests on the assumption that God *wants* us to be monogamous,
Darwin (1871) hypothesized that an even sex ratio at maturity evolved as an
adaptive response to the *fact* of monogamy. Darwin (1874) withdrew that
hypothesis, but never explained why. He may have been moved by the fact
that present-day human populations are often polygynous and that many of our
ape relatives are too. If all these contemporary groups have even sex ratios, but
only a few are monogamous, an inference can be drawn concerning the mating
patterns and sex ratios found in ancestral populations. As shown in simplified
form in Figure 4, the inference is that an even sex ratio predated the evolution of
monogamy in the human lineage; monogamy was a Johnny-come-lately (Sober
2011). This strategy of ancestral state reconstruction also justifies the claim that
the vertebrate eye gradually evolved from simpler precursors; the eyes found in
contemporary *non*-vertebrates underwrite inferences concerning the eyes that
existed in the lineage leading to vertebrates now.[58]

Adaptive hypotheses often address the question of why a trait varies across the
species in a given taxonomic group, rather than focusing on the specific trait
a single species exhibits. For example, Clutton-Brock and Harvey (1977) gath-
ered data on the average body sizes of males and females in several primate
species. Males are on average larger than females in each species, but the degree

---

[58] For discussion of how parsimony and likelihood guide inferences of ancestral character states,
see Sober (2015).

of size difference varies across species. The authors noticed that the degree of size dimorphism between the sexes is associated with the "socionomic" sex ratio (the sex ratio in mating groups).[59] The more that females outnumber males in mating groups, the greater the size difference between the sexes tends to be. The authors took this observed association to be evidence for sexual selection. When males compete with each other for access to females, a male can gain an advantage over other males by being bigger. Clutton-Brock and Harvey's argument can be put into a likelihood format by considering two hypotheses:

- In primates, size dimorphism between the sexes evolved by a process of sexual selection in which the optimal male body size in a species is positively correlated with the degree of female bias in the socionomic sex ratio in that species.
- In primates, the size dimorphism between the sexes in a species and the socionomic sex ratio in that species evolved independently of each other.

The sexual selection hypothesis confers a higher probability on the observed association than the independence hypothesis does. This argument can be elaborated by taking account of the fact that contemporary primates have a most recent common ancestor, with the two hypotheses disagreeing about the processes that caused the descendants of that common ancestor to diverge from each other (Sober and Orzack 2003). A further wrinkle is that the selection hypothesis assumes that the dimorphism in body size in a primate lineage evolved as an adaptive response to the socionomic sex ratio already in place. This claim about chronological order can be checked by reconstructing the character states of ancestors, as just explained in connection with Darwin's (1871) hypothesis about sex ratio and monogamy.

Biologists are often able to assemble observational evidence concerning which traits are optimal for an organism. Here's an example. Crows on the west coast of Canada eat whelks. To break the shell, a crow carries a whelk aloft and drops it on the rocks. What is the optimal height from which crows should drop whelks? Zach (1978) addressed this question by taking the benefit to a crow as its success rate in breaking shells and the cost as the energy spent flying. If a crow flies too low, it needs to drop the whelk more than once to get it to break; if the crow flies too high, it wastes effort. Zach computed the total vertical distances that each of numerous whelks were carried before they broke. Whelks dropped from 3 meters or less needed to be dropped again, whereas whelks dropped from 5 to 15 meters did not. Zach concluded that 5 meters is the

---

[59] Don't confuse the sex ratio in *mating groups* with the *population* sex ratio. It's possible for a population to have an even sex ratio even though each mating group has the same biased sex ratio.

optimal drop height. He observed that crows average 5.2 meters. Notice that the *optimal* trait is not identified by simply assuming that the *observed* trait average is optimal; that would be empty.

Zach's optimality argument does not mention the history of the trait's evolution, but biologists often take the two to be connected. One hypothesis to consider is this. If 5 meters is the optimum, then natural selection will cause the mean of the population to move toward that value. This does not explain why organisms in the population now vary, nor why the present average is 5.2 rather than 5.0 (Orzack and Sober 1994), but the fact that the observed mean is close to the optimum suggests that natural selection influenced the trait's evolution. This all sounds like good news for the evolutionary hypothesis, but there is a fly in the ointment. As Zach notes, individual crows modify their whelk-dropping behavior by learning what works and what does not. Arguably, what evolved is not a specific strategy for breaking whelks, but some more general learning mechanism. Still, this example illustrates how biological optima can be ascertained empirically.

4.12 What If the Problem of God's Goals Can Be Solved?

Suppose, contrary to what I have argued, that there are observations that favor the God hypothesis over the hypothesis of natural selection. Perhaps we can't assign point values to either likelihood, but suppose we can assert, with justification, that there is a likelihood inequality.

This supposition doesn't get the design argument out of the woods. The reason is that if there are observations of the type just described, there are other possible observations that would have the opposite evidential significance. This is an instance of a symmetry entailed by the law of likelihood, described in §2.8 and mentioned earlier in this section. For example, if you think that a trait's being complex and adaptive favors God over natural selection, then you are obliged to conclude that a trait that is neither complex nor adaptive would favor natural selection over God. In fact, biologists observe both types of traits.

Suppose you have two observations (O_1 and O_2) and want to evaluate whether they together favor the God hypothesis over the hypothesis of natural selection. If the two observations are probabilistically independent of each other, conditional on each of the two hypotheses under test, you can write:

$$\frac{\Pr(O_1 \& O_2 \mid God)}{\Pr(O_1 \& O_2 \mid Selection)} = \frac{\Pr(O_1 \mid God)}{\Pr(O_1 \mid Selection)} \times \frac{\Pr(O_2 \mid God)}{\Pr(O_2 \mid Selection)}.$$

If each observation favors God over selection, so does their conjunction; there is no need to know the numerical value of any of these ratios to say this. That is what happened when Susan got two positive tuberculosis test results in §2.7. The situation is messier if the first ratio on the right-hand side is greater than one while the second is less. This "mixed news" will fail to deliver a victory to either hypothesis over the other if you can't say whether the product of these two ratios is greater than one.

Maybe this Gordian knot can be cut. Notice that if $Pr(O_1 \mid God)$ is zero, it won't matter what the value of $Pr(O_2 \mid God)$ is; there is no way that God can have a higher likelihood than selection, regardless of which other observations you consider. A symmetrical point applies if you rewrite the foregoing equation by putting selection in the numerator and God in the denominator. Now, if $Pr(O_2 \mid Selection)$ is zero, there is no way that selection can have the higher likelihood, regardless of which other observations you mention. Given this, it is no surprise that friends of evolutionary theory have searched for observations that the God hypothesis says cannot happen while friends of the God hypothesis have searched for observations that evolutionary theory says cannot happen. The argument from evil, in its strong form, is often placed under the first heading. I now want to explore an attempt to find an observation that falls under the second (or comes close).

4.13 Irreducible Complexity

Michael Behe, in his book *Darwin's Black Box*, argues that irreducibly complex biological systems constitute an insurmountable problem for evolutionary biology. Behe defines this concept as follows:

> ... a single system composed of several well-matched interacting parts that contribute to the basic function, wherein the removal of any one of the parts causes the system to effectively cease functioning. (Behe 1996, p. 39)

Behe's concept is close to what I talked about earlier under the heading of "delicacy." Behe is therefore on the same page as Paley, though his examples are different. Behe's favorites, unknown to Paley, include the bacterial flagellum and the biochemical mechanisms that cause blood coagulation.

Behe develops his thesis that irreducible complexity is a stake through the heart of evolutionary theory by distinguishing "direct" and "indirect" pathways. With respect to the first, he argues that:

> An irreducibly complex system cannot be produced directly (that is, by continuously improving the initial function, which continues to work by the same mechanism) by slight successive modifications of a precursor system, because any precursor to an irreducibly complex system that is missing a part is by definition nonfunctional. (Behe 1996, p. 39)

As for indirect pathways, Behe says this:

> One cannot definitively rule out the possibility of an indirect, circuitous route. As the complexity of the interacting system increases, though, the likelihood of such an indirect route drops precipitously. (Behe 1996, p. 40)

Behe's point here is not just that the probability of indirect circuitous routes goes down the more complex the structure is. That might be expected, and would be no threat to evolutionary biology. As explained in §2.2, an improbable event can have a high probability of happening if you try and try again. Rather, the word "precipitously" signals Behe's belief that the drop is so severe that one can no longer believe that the structure evolved in that way. Behe's thesis is that irreducible complexity cannot arise by the direct route, and is so improbable by an indirect route that that second option should also be rejected.

What does "part" mean in Behe's definition of irreducible complexity? Every functional structure is irreducibly complex relative to one way of dividing it into parts, and it fails to be irreducibly complex relative to another. If you view the many molecules that make up an eye as different parts, then the eye is not irreducibly complex. However, if you take the retina, the cornea, the optic nerve, and so on to be its parts, it is. This puzzle about "parts" leaves Behe's claim open to obvious counterexample. Suppose the four legs of a horse are the four parts of a system whose function is walking or running. Take one away and the horse can't walk or run. However, this doesn't prevent the tetrapod structure from evolving gradually from ancestors that had no limbs. It did, but not by adding one leg at a time. There also is the question of what "function" means in Behe's definition of irreducible complexity. Mammals have two eyes; if one is removed, the organism can still see, but cannot do stereopsis (depth perception underwritten by binocular vision). Is this visual system irreducibly complex? I'll assume in what follows that these two problems can be solved.

Behe's definition of irreducible complexity is represented in Figure 5. What does that definition entail concerning whether gradual step-by-step natural selection can cause an irreducibly complex structure to evolve? If natural selection controls the evolutionary process occurring in a lineage, structures with higher fitness increase in frequency and structures with lower fitness decline. In a selection process, what matters is *fitness*; there is no requirement that a structure's evolution be governed by how well it contributes to a single, unchanging *function*. In fact, the evolution of many structures has involved *function switching*, wherein the structure starts evolving because it performs one function, but then continues to evolve because it performs another.

For an example, consider the insect wing. Its present function is to allow organisms to fly or glide, but how can gradual natural selection get this structure

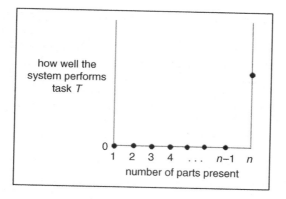

Figure 5 If there are *n* parts that a system now has, and the present function of the system is to perform task *T*, how well would the system perform that task if it had 1, or 2, . . ., or *n*−1, or all *n* parts present? If the system is irreducibly complex, the functionality is zero unless all parts are in place.

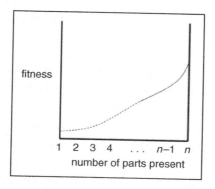

Figure 6 A model of the evolution of insect wings in which wings start to evolve as thermoregulators and then continue to evolve because they facilitate gliding and flying. The function of the structure changes, but there is steadily increasing fitness along the way. The two stages of the structure's evolution are represented by a broken line and a solid line.

Table 2 The fitness of the system depends on which A and B parts it has. Suppose the system now has three A parts ($A_1A_2A_3$) and no B parts. It is irreducibly complex, since if A_3 is removed, its fitness plunges from 0.7 to 0, and suppose that the same is true if A_2 or A_1 is removed. Nonetheless, $A_1A_2A_3$ can evolve one step at a time, starting with A_1 and no Bs, with ever increasing fitness, by a ∩-shaped trajectory.

	A_1	A_1A_2	$A_1A_2A_3$
B_1B_2	0.3	0.4	0.5
B_1	0.2	0	0.6
no Bs	0.1	0	0.7

to evolve if 1% (or 2%, or 3%, or . . .) of a wing doesn't allow the organism to fly or glide at all? To see how, consider the fact that many insects now have small wing buds that don't allow the organism to fly or glide. These insects turn their buds toward or away from the sun to regulate body temperature. Kingsolver and Koehl (1985) hypothesize that insect wings started evolving because they were thermal regulators and then, after wings got bigger, they continued to evolve because they then facilitated flight. In this scenario, fitness steadily increases as wing size increases, even though small wings provide zero flight. I discussed this hypothesis in Sober (2008, p. 161), not to defend its correctness, but to illustrate a conceptual point. The wings that insects now have conform to what you see in Figure 5, but that is irrelevant. What is relevant is the situation depicted in Figure 6. Figure 5 is about *function* whereas Figure 6 is about *fitness*. If the Kingsolver and Koehl hypothesis is correct, insect wings did not evolve by Behe's "direct pathway." However, that is no reason to think that their hypothesis is too unlikely to be worth considering.[60]

A second deviation from Behe's direct pathway is depicted in Table 2.[61] Suppose the organisms in a present population all have a structure that has three A parts ($A_1A_2A_3$) but no B parts, and that this structure is irreducibly complex. It nonetheless can evolve step by step, starting with just A_1, by adding B parts, then adding A parts, and then subtracting B parts. Natural selection causes those changes at every step. The biologist Allen Orr (1997) gives a nice example of this pattern:

> The transformation of air bladders into lungs that allowed animals to breathe atmospheric oxygen was initially just advantageous: such beasts could explore open niches – like dry land – that were unavailable to their lung-less peers. But as evolution built on this adaptation (modifying limbs for

---

[60] Jantzen (2014) discusses a different hypothesis about the evolution of insect wings to make the same point.

[61] I presented this argument in Sober (2008, pp. 162–163) by using a genetic example involving epistasis. It was inspired by a mortarless stone arch that Cairn-Smith (1982, pp. 93–99) described.

walking, for instance), we grew thoroughly terrestrial and lungs, consequently, are no longer luxuries – they are essential. The punch-line is, I think, obvious: although this process is thoroughly Darwinian, we are often left with a system that is irreducibly complex.

Here the process of adding and subtracting takes place with the evolving system's fitness determined by its contribution to a single unchanging functional task – extracting oxygen from the environment. The lineage evolves from gills only, to gills+lungs, and then to lungs only.

I hope it now is clear why irreducibly complex structures can gradually evolve, one part at a time, when there is function switching or adding and subtracting. These may be "indirect" pathways in Behe's terminology, but they are not far-fetched. Still, the fact that these scenarios are *possible* leaves substantive work for biologists to do; they have the job of reconstructing the details of how different irreducibly complex systems *actually* evolved. These reconstructions must be evaluated on a case-by-case basis. Irreducibly complex structures present interesting research *projects*, not in-principle *problems* that evolutionary biology cannot solve.

4.14 Concluding Comments

I argued in this section that the likelihood version of the biological design argument is deeply flawed because there is no telling whether the likelihood of the God hypothesis is big, or small, or somewhere in between, given the features of organisms that we observe. This is enough to undermine the likelihood argument, regardless of whether hypotheses in evolutionary biology do a better job of conferring probabilities on observations. I argued, though, that they do.

The next section is on the fine-tuning argument. You may be guessing that I there harp exclusively on the point I have belabored in this one – that the obscurity of God's goals makes trouble for design arguments. If so, you are in for a surprise.

5 The Fine-Tuning Argument

The laws of physics contain constants whose values can be accurately measured by assembling observations.[62] Given those measured values, it has been claimed that our present physical theories have a remarkable counterfactual

---

[62] To see what a constant is, consider Newton's universal law of gravitation:

$$\text{For any two objects } a \text{ and } b, \; F(a,b) \;=\; G\frac{M(a)M(b)}{[R(a,b)]^2}.$$

That is, for any two objects, the gravitational force that each exerts on the other equals G times the product of their masses divided by the square of the distance between them. G is the gravitational constant.

consequence: if the values of those constants were more than a little different from their actual values, it would be impossible for life to exist in our universe. The fine-tuning argument (FTA) accepts the measured values and the counterfactual consequence and attempts to parlay them into an argument for the existence of God. My focus here is on whether that parlaying succeeds.

I suggested in Section 3 that the strongest version of this argument aims to establish a likelihood inequality:

(IN)   Pr(the value of physical constant x is in W | God set the value of x & W is narrow) >
         Pr(the value of physical constant x is in W | a mindless chance process set the value of x & W is narrow).[63]

Here W is the window of all and only the values of constant x that permit life to exist. It would be better to write "W is narrow" as a subscript of the probability function, since it is an assumption, not a supposition (in the sense of §2.3).

By using the IN inequality to formulate the FTA, I'm focusing on what the argument says about the value of a single physical constant, but that's a simplification. You need to consider whether life could exist if *each* of the constants were changed while the values of the others remained the same, but varying pairs of constants while holding the others fixed matters too; ditto for triples, quadruples, and so on. A further complication is that some constants depend on others, and the FTA is often presented by discussing dimensionless ratios of constants. My simplification is harmless, however, given the arguments I want to make.

The chance hypothesis discussed in the FTA is something of a concoction; it isn't part of current physics in anything like the way that hypotheses about natural selection are part of evolutionary biology. For this reason, even if the God hypothesis turns out to be more likely than the chance hypothesis in the FTA, you might feel that that doesn't show that the God hypothesis is any good at all, since the chance hypothesis in this argument seems to have been pulled out of thin air. Regardless of whether you think this, the FTA is interesting, on several fronts.

In what follows, I explore three objections to the FTA. The first claims that the IN inequality is untrue because the likelihood of the chance hypothesis either makes no sense or is arbitrary (§5.1). The second grants that the inequality makes sense, but argues that there is no telling whether it is true (§5.2). The third concedes that the inequality is true, but contends that it is the wrong proposition to consider (§5.3–§5.7).

---

[63] Le Poidevin (1996, p. 57) criticizes the FTA on the grounds that "it makes no sense to talk of the probability of a life-sustaining universe in the absence of God." I don't like catchalls either, which is why I have not represented the alternative to God as a catchall.

5.1 A Mathematical Problem

McGrew, McGrew, and Vestrup (2001, p. 1028) describe a mathematical problem for the fine-tuning argument that they say "may well be insuperable." They question whether

> Pr(the value of constant x falls in window W | the value of x was set by a mindless chance process & W is the narrow window of values in which life is possible)

makes sense, given the supposition that it is logically possible for the constant in question to have any non-negative value. Chance hypotheses often postulate flat probability distributions for all possible values. However, if the chance hypothesis in the FTA is understood in this way, it is not "normalizable," meaning that the probabilities assigned to the infinitely many nonoverlapping and exhaustive finite value intervals do not sum to one. Either each interval receives an assignment of zero, in which case the sum is zero, or each receives the same positive value, in which case the sum is infinite. Neither of these is acceptable.

This problem can be solved, as McGrew et al. (2001, p. 1033) note, by dropping the requirement that the probability distribution be flat. For example, you could assign a probability of $\frac{1}{2}$ to the parameter's having a value between 0 and 10, a probability of $\frac{1}{4}$ to its having a value between 10 and 20, and so on. Now each finite interval receives a nonzero probability, and the infinite series $\frac{1}{2}$, $\frac{1}{4}$, $\frac{1}{8}$, $\frac{1}{16}$... sums to one. The problem of normalizability has now been solved, but, according to McGrew et al., a new problem arises – how "to choose, without arbitrariness," which distribution or family of distributions "is the 'right' one." Notice that this is a problem for the chance hypothesis, not for the God hypothesis.[64]

How should you understand McGrew et al.'s demand that a justification be provided for choosing a single distribution or a single family of distributions as the "right one" for the chance hypothesis to deploy? If this means that you need to show that that choice has a higher probability under the chance hypothesis than any other choice has, then I agree that the demand cannot be satisfied. However, there is another angle I want to explore.[65]

---

[64] Collins (2003) proposes to solve this problem by having the chance hypothesis be a step function that postulates a single, finitely wide, flat island of positive values that is much wider than the one postulated by the God hypothesis. See Jantzen (2014, pp. 287–290) for criticisms. Collins's step function differs dramatically from what is usually meant by chance. Collins (2009, pp. 244ff.) represents the chance hypothesis in the same way.

[65] My thanks to Mike Steel for suggesting this approach.

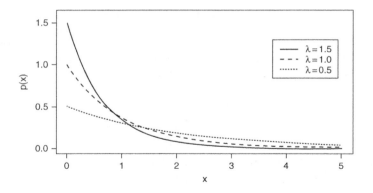

Figure 7 Three exponential probability density functions

I want to consider an infinite sequence of probability distributions. Each is flatter than the one before, but there is no flattest distribution, and none is absolutely flat (since that would violate normalizability). The tool I'll use is the family of exponential distributions. Exponential distributions have the form:

$$F(x; \lambda) = \lambda e^{-\lambda x} (x \geq 0),$$

where e is the base of the natural logarithm, λ is the probability density[66] at $x = 0$, and $\frac{1}{\lambda}$ is the mean value of the distribution. The function is fixed by providing a value for λ. Figure 7 depicts three exponential functions that use different values for λ. The area under each curve is one (so each is normalizable). Notice that as the value of λ declines, the functions get flatter and flatter.

When the God hypothesis is compared with each of the chance hypotheses that takes the form of an exponential probability distribution, there are two relevant facts:

---

[66] Probability *density* and probability are different. To understand the former, suppose a parameter must fall somewhere in the interval [0,10], and you think that all equally wide windows in that interval are equiprobable. For example, you think that the probability of the value's falling between 2 and 7 is the same as the probability of its falling between 3 and 8, and that both equal 0.5, and you also think that the probability of its falling between 6 and 8 is the same as its falling between 1 and 3, with both equaling 0.2. The concept of probability density allows a general rule to be stated for computing these and all the other probabilities for all the intervals in [0,10]. Each point value in the interval has a probability *density* of $\frac{1}{10}$ (even though its probability is 0). The probability of falling in an interval inside of [0,10] is the width of that interval times the density. So the probability of falling in [2,7] is $5(\frac{1}{10})$, and the probability of falling in [6,8] is $2(\frac{1}{10})$. Probability densities, unlike probabilities, can have values greater than 1. To see why, consider a continuous parameter whose value must fall between 3.3 and 3.8. A flat distribution for the density means that its value at each point in the interval is 2. The density idea also applies to nonflat distributions like the exponential curves depicted in Figure 7. The probability that a curve assigns to x falling in a window W that runs from $x = a$ to $x = b$ is the area under the curve between those x values; to compute that area you need the probability density of the curve at each x value in W.

(X₁)   For every exponential function f and every finite width w that the window W of life-permitting values might have, Pr(constant x is in W | God set the value of x & W has width w) > Pr(constant x is in W | function f set the value of x & W has width w).

Assuming that God is life-loving (more on this soon), proposition X₁ is true because the God hypothesis has a likelihood of 1, but exponential functions never do. Although this point holds no matter how narrow or wide the finite life-permitting window W is, the width of the window does matter; it affects the value of the likelihood *ratio*, as follows:

(X₂)   For each exponential function f, the likelihood ratio of God to f approaches infinity as the width of window W approaches zero.

The likelihood ratio is a standard measure of how strongly an observation favors one hypothesis over another. The narrower the window of life-permitting values, the more the evidence favors God over any given exponential function.

Critics of the FTA sometimes complain that it is unclear why we should be impressed that the life-permitting window of values for the physical constants is "very small" (McGrew et al. 2001, p. 1032; Colyvan, Garfield, and Priest 2005, p. 327; Jantzen 2014, p. 294). After all, every finitely wide window is equally tiny when compared with the infinitely wide range of logically possible values. These critics demand that defenders of the FTA say how small is small enough for the FTA to succeed. The framework described here entails that this complaint is doubly mistaken. First, if the *narrow width of the window* were the observation that the FTA says discriminates between God and chance, the critics would be right; it can't be true that *all* possible finite widths favor God over chance,[67] and so the FTA would be obliged to say which widths do the trick. However, the width of the window is not the *observation* considered. The observation cited in proposition X₁ is the fact that constant x falls in window W; the width of W is on the right side of the conditional probability signs, not the left. Second, the ratio result X₂ shows that the narrowness of the window *does* affect how much the observation favors God over a given exponential function. There is no line between widths that are too big and widths that are sufficiently small, nor does the FTA need to say that there is; the difference is a matter of degree.

Although I've formulated the FTA by using the family of exponential functions to codify what "chance" means, my argument can be extended to probability distributions that are not exponential. So long as the likelihood of

---

[67] This is an instance of the symmetry attaching to the law of likelihood noted in §2.8.

God is one, and the likelihood of the alternative hypothesis is less than one, the likelihood inequality is in the bag. This will be true of many chance distributions. Getting the likelihood ratio to increase as the width of the window narrows is a further issue, but that idea also applies to many chance distributions that aren't exponential.

My abandoning the requirement of uniqueness – the requirement that there must be a single distribution that codifies what "chance" means in the FTA – was prefigured by the discussion in §3.5 of Arbuthnot and Bernouilli. Arbuthnot's chance hypothesis postulates a flat probability distribution wherein the probability of a birth's being a boy is $\frac{1}{2}$ and the probability of its being a girl is also $\frac{1}{2}$. Bernouilli's hypothesis says that the probabilities are $\frac{18}{35}$ and $\frac{17}{35}$. Arbuthnot's is a chance hypothesis and so is Bernouilli's. True, Arbuthnot's is more chancy because it is flatter, but it makes sense to consider them both as competitors to the God hypothesis. For similar reasons, we should consider many chancy hypotheses in the FTA, even if none of them is perfectly flat. The alternative – of refusing to consider any of them, because none has a unique claim to the title of "chance" – strikes me as misguided. I conclude that if the FTA is flawed, the flaw is not to be found in the mathematics.

5.2 The Problem of God's Goals

Although I argued in the previous section that the obscurity of God's goals is a powerful objection to biological design arguments, this objection may seem less pressing when it comes to the FTA. After all, if God is life-loving and sets the values of the physical constants, then God will surely choose values that are compatible with life, and this can be seen without fussing over any biological details. But *is* God life-loving?[68] If God loves life, why is there so little of it in the universe? Here one finds a parallel with the problem of evil. As noted earlier, the problem of evil isn't to explain why there is some evil rather than none at all. Rather, the problem is to explain why there is so much evil rather than less. The present question is: why is there so little life rather than more (Everitt 2003)? An independently justified auxiliary assumption is needed (§4.3).[69] It's true that some dog lovers own just one, but that doesn't answer the question about God.

---

[68] Narveson (2003) argues that we can't know whether Pr(life exists | God made the universe) is big, middling, or small.

[69] Collins (2009) disagrees with this criticism of the FTA when he writes that:

> As Richard Swinburne has argued (2004, pp. 99–106), since God is perfectly good, omniscient, omnipotent, and perfectly free, the only motivation God has for bringing about one state of affairs instead of another is its relative (probable) contribution to the overall moral and aesthetic value of reality. Simple forms of life, such as bacteria, do

Even if you assume that God would ensure that life exists, there is another problem. The FTA takes the laws of physics as given and gives God the job of choosing values for the constants in those laws. That is, the likelihood version of the FTA considers the following probability:

Pr(the constant x in law L has a value that falls in window W | L is true & God chose a value for x in L & W is the narrow window of values for x in L that permit life to exist).

Why is the truth of law L on the right-hand side of the conditional probability sign rather than on the left? Don't friends of the FTA think that God chose the laws? If so, the probability to consider is this one:

Pr(law L is true & the constant x in L has a value that falls in window W | God chose the laws of nature and values for the constants in those laws & W is the narrow window of values for x in L that permit life to exist).

This raises a new question: why didn't God choose laws that permit life to exist across a much wider range of possible values for their constants? If the laws had been different, the quantity of life in the universe could have been the same without God needing to fine-tune (Monton 2006, p. 421; Weisberg 2010, p. 434).[70]

---

not seem in and of themselves to contribute to the overall moral value of reality, although it is possible that they might contribute to its overall aesthetic value. On the other hand, embodied moral agents seem to allow for the realization of unique types of value (p. 254).

My response is that the assumption that God, if there is such a being, must be all-PKG requires an independent justification if the design argument is to be part of *natural* theology (§4.10).

On the next page, Collins (2009, p. 255) agrees that the FTA needs to show that it is plausible to suppose that God wants there to be life. However, he says this requirement would be satisfied if the hypothetical "unembodied being" he discusses were to be in a situation of complete ignorance about God's goals. This commits Collins to the thesis that the FTA can succeed even if that hypothetical being is completely in the dark about God's goals *and so are we*. Collins says his point here draws on the idea that there are two strategies that theists can use in replying to an argument for atheism that is based on the existence of evil (§4.10). A *theodicy* seeks to explain why God wants to allow evil to exist; a *defense* tries to disarm the argument for atheism merely by showing that we can't tell what God wants. I agree that the fact that we are ignorant can disarm arguments that mistakenly assume that we have knowledge, but it's hard to see how ignorance of God's goals can make the FTA work, especially if the argument is a likelihood argument – a point on which Collins and I concur. Collins uses an epistemic interpretation of probability, but that, I think, doesn't help.

[70] This problem resembles one described in §4.4. A biological design argument can't simply assume that God wanted there to be vertebrates, and then address the question of why God gave them camera eyes.

5.3 The Problem of Observation Selection Effects

Suppose the objections to the FTA discussed in the previous section fail, and that the God hypothesis *does* make it highly probable that there will be life in the universe. Even granting this, there is another objection to the FTA to consider.

I argued in §4.2 that Duhem's thesis is relevant to assessing likelihoods. Competing hypotheses often do not confer probabilities on the observations unless auxiliary assumptions are appended. If you think the oatmeal breakfast order favors the hypothesis that Jane placed the order over the hypothesis that Joe did, you must be making assumptions about Jane's and Joe's goals. These assumptions are about the two people, not about the process by which you came to observe the breakfast order, but sometimes facts about the process of observation are crucial to figuring out whether your observations favor one hypothesis over another.

To see why, consider a famous example described by Eddington (1939). You use a net to fish in a lake and observe that all the fish in your net are more than 10 inches long (call this proposition *O*). You then consider two hypotheses about the lake:

(H1)   All the fish in the lake are more than 10 inches long.
(H2)   Half the fish in the lake are more than 10 inches long.

You initially think that *O* favors H_1 over H_2 (in the sense of the law of likelihood), but then you notice that the net you used has holes that are big enough to ensure that fish less than 10 inches long will easily escape. Call this proposition *B*, for big. This discovery leads you to revise your assessment. You reason that the observation doesn't favor H_1 over H_2, since $\Pr(O \mid H_1 \& B) = \Pr(O \mid H_2 \& B)$. Given the construction of the net, the probability of proposition *O* is the same, regardless of whether H_1 or H_2 is true (Sober 2003, 2009). Your net gave rise to an *observation selection effect* (an OSE). Had you used a net with small holes, you could have avoided this problem.

The OSE engendered by the net with big holes is there whether you know it or not. If you aren't sure what sort of net you used, you might assign a degree of belief *p* to your having used a net with big holes and a degree of belief $1-p$ to your having used a net with small holes (call this proposition *S*). You then would conclude that your evidence favors H_1 over H_2, since

$$\Pr(O \mid H_1) = \Pr(O \mid H_1 \& B)p + \Pr(O \mid H_1 \& S)(1-p) >$$
$$\Pr(O \mid H_2) = \Pr(O \mid H_2 \& B)p + \Pr(O \mid H_2 \& S)(1-p).^{71}$$

---

[71] This inequality is true because $0 < p < 1$, $\Pr(O \mid H_1 \& B) = \Pr(O \mid H_2 \& B)$, and $\Pr(O \mid H_1 \& S) > \Pr(O \mid H_2 \& S)$.

This is how a subjective Bayesian would assess the problem (Monton 2006), but the OSE concept requires a different analysis. The physical facts about the net you *actually* used induced an OSE. Your *uncertainty* about those facts is irrelevant.

The role played by the process of observation in interpreting evidence is made explicit in the following *improved law of likelihood* (ILL):

(ILL)   Given that P is true, where P is a proposition describing the process by which the observation was obtained, observation O favors hypothesis H_1 over hypothesis H_2 if and only if $\Pr(O \mid H_1 \& P) > \Pr(O \mid H_2 \& P)$.[72]

Since H_1 and H_2 are suppositions whereas P is an assumption (§2.3), it would be better to have the ILL say that $\Pr_p(O \mid H_1) > \Pr_p(O \mid H_2)$.

The FTA asserts the likelihood inequality IN, but once you use the improved law of likelihood (ILL) and take account of your process of observation, it turns out that the relevant likelihoods are equal. Instead of IN, you should focus on

(EQ)   Pr(you observe that the value of physical constant x is in W | God set the value of x & W is narrow & P) = Pr(you observe that the value of physical constant x is in W | a mindless chance process set the value of x & W is narrow & P).[73]

P describes your process of observation. Once again, it might be better to place P as a subscript on the probability function in EQ, since P is an assumption, not a supposition.

---

[72] Kotzen (2012, p. 835) prefers a different reformulation of the law of likelihood:

> The fact that observation O was collected through a process of observation characterized by P is evidence for H_1 over H_2 if and only if $\Pr(O\&P \mid H_1) > \Pr(O\&P \mid H_2)$.

I think this principle and the ILL address different problems. Kotzen's says when the conjunction $O\&P$ provides discriminating evidence; the ILL says when O provides discriminating evidence, given that P is true. These are different, just as the following two questions are:

- Does observing a black raven confirm the hypothesis that all ravens are black?
- If you sample at random from the ravens, and the raven you sample is observed to be black, does that observation confirm the hypothesis that all ravens are black?

The first question is hard to answer, since no sampling process is mentioned; the second is easier. See Horwich (1982) for discussion. Kotzen's principle does not mention the process by which the conjunction $O\&P$ came to be observed. This is needed (as cases of publication bias reveal), and adding it will, I think, lead you gently back to the ILL. Jantzen (2014) also discusses Kotzen's proposal.

[73] Notice that the evidence statement in EQ (the statements on the left side of the conditional probability sign) isn't just the claim that constant x falls in window W; the evidence is the logically stronger claim that you *observe* that constant x does so. Here again, I abide by the principle of total evidence (§2.9). Sometimes it makes no difference whether you use a weaker or a stronger formulation of the evidence; you get the same answer either way. But OSEs often need to be analyzed by using the stronger formulation of the evidence at hand.

The shift from EQ to IN is sanctioned by the weak anthropic principle (Earman 1987), which Carter (1974) formulated like this: "what we can expect to observe must be restricted by the conditions necessary for our presence as observers."

The EQ equality represents the fact that your process of observation has induced an OSE. But what is it about your process of observation that has had that consequence? That is, what should be substituted for the letter P in the EQ proposition? One possibility (to be refined shortly) is the fact that you are alive. Given that you are alive, the probability of your observing that the constants are right is the same, regardless of whether the God hypothesis or the chance hypothesis is true. Nothing changes if you are unsure about whether you are alive. Studying philosophy may have led you to wonder whether you are a living thing, a lifeless robot, or an incorporeal being (Weisberg 2005). Your uncertainty does not matter. The fact is that you are alive. You drag that fact behind you like a net.[74]

5.4 The Firing Squad

The similarity of fishing and fine-tuning may seem compelling, but a clever example, described by John Leslie (1989), appears to throw doubt on the analysis just given. You are brought before a firing squad. They fire, and then you are surprised to find that you are alive and unscathed. You conclude that your being alive is evidence that favors the first of the following hypotheses over the second:

(H3)   The firing squad decided to spare you.
(H4)   The firing squad decided to kill you.

It seems obvious that there is a likelihood inequality here:

Pr(you are alive | H_3) > Pr(you are alive | H_4).

It also seems obvious that this inequality should not be replaced with the following equality:

Pr(you are alive | H_3 & you are alive) = Pr(you are alive | H_4 & you are alive).

This equality is true but irrelevant; there is no OSE at work. Leslie's example shows that it is a delicate matter to decide which proposition to use in

---

[74] If the observation described in proposition EQ fails to favor God over chance, perhaps there is a different observation that does so. The laws of physics permit life to exist only within a very narrow range of parameter values. Does that fact favor God over chance? This suggestion is not undermined by an OSE (Roberts 2012; McGrew 2016), but it does face the problem that God's goals are obscure (§5.2).

describing the process of observation in EQ. It also raises the question of whether fine-tuning resembles Eddington's fishing more than it resembles Leslie's firing squad.

5.5 The OSE Concept

It helps to analyze this problem if you use time indices for the different propositions that might characterize a Source at t_1, an Observational Outcome at t_3, and the Process that occurs in between at t_2 (Sober 2009).[75] The three times need not be temporal instants; they can be disjoint temporal intervals. Here are the descriptors I want to consider for the three examples:

Fishing: At t_1 all of the fish in the lake are more than 10 inches long or only 50% of them are (and the percentage remains the same thereafter). At t_2 you put your net in the lake. At t_3 you observe that all the fish in the net are longer than 10 inches.

Fine-Tuning: At t_1 the constants have their values set, either by God or by chance (and the values remain the same thereafter). At t_2 you are alive. At t_3 you observe that the constants are right.

Firing Squad: At t_1 the firing squad decides whether it will spare you or kill you when they fire (and the decision remains in place thereafter). At t_2 you are alive and the firing squad fires just after t_2. At t_3 you observe that you are alive.

I'm assuming that what happens at one time can affect the probability of what happens next, but does not necessitate it. In each example, there are two hypotheses about what happens at t_1. At t_3, there is a single observational outcome.

Besides introducing temporal indices and requiring that the descriptors that characterize one time not necessitate what happens later, I need to add a further constraint on how the process of observation should be taken into account in assessing an observation's bearing on competing hypotheses. This constraint can be identified by considering the children's game of Telephone. Ruby whispers a word to Ezra, then Ezra whispers to Lilah what he thinks Ruby said. Lilah then whispers what she thinks she heard to a fourth child, and so on. The game ends, typically in giggles, when the last child in the chain reports what he or she heard and Ruby then tells everyone what she said in the first place. For simplicity, I focus on the three children mentioned, and I suppose that each must choose between "apple" and "orange" as the word that he or she

---

[75] My discussion of OSEs in this section adds to what I said in Sober (2009), and both depart in important ways from what I suggested in Sober (2003).

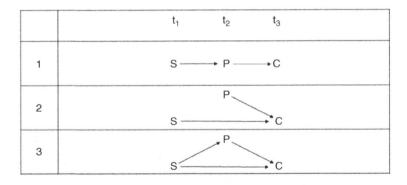

Figure 8 Three possible casual relationships linking Source (S), Process (P), and Observation (O)

will say. Even though transmission is subject to error, Lilah's hearing "apple" at t_3 is evidence concerning what Ruby said at t_1, since

Pr(Lilah hears "apple" at t_3 | Ruby said "apple" at t_1) >
Pr(Lilah hears "apple" at t_3 | Ruby said "orange" at t_1).

This claim about evidence is not undermined by the fact that a probabilistic equality results if you insert information about what Ezra said at t_2:

Pr(Lilah hears "apple" at t_3 | Ruby said "apple" at t_1 & Ezra said "apple" at t_2) =
Pr(Lilah hears "apple" at t_3 | Ruby said "orange" at t_1 & Ezra said "apple" at t_2).

This equality is true but irrelevant when it comes to deciding whether Lilah's impression at t_3 is evidence concerning what Ruby said at t_1. Ezra at t_2 is part of the process by which Ruby at t_1 affects Lilah at t_3, but you should not consider what Ezra says in deciding whether Lilah's state is evidence concerning what Ruby said.

The game of Telephone suggests a general point. Consider Figure 8. In pattern 1, S causes O only by way of causing the intermediate process P, and the probability that O occurs, given the process at work, is the same regardless of what state the source S occupies. In pattern 2, S and P are probabilistically independent causes of O. In 3, there are two pathways from S to O, one of which passes through P. In assessing whether observation O provides evidence about source S, you should take process P into account if the problem conforms to pattern 2 or 3, but not if it has pattern 1. Telephone exhibits pattern 1, but fishing, fine-tuning, and the firing squad exhibit pattern 2 or 3.

5.6 Fishing, Fine-Tuning, and the Firing Squad

Tables 3, 4, and 5 each describe the probability of an observational outcome conditional on different hypotheses about the source and different propositions about the observational process. Each table has two columns, but only the left-hand column is relevant to the likelihood analysis, since I assume that the propositions that label that column are true and the ones that label the right-hand column are false. I include those right-hand columns for a reason I soon explain. With respect to the left-hand columns, fine-tuning resembles fishing, not the firing squad.

Why do fine-tuning and the firing squad differ with respect to their left-hand columns? In fine-tuning, if you are alive at t_2, the constants must be right at t_1, t_2, and t_3, and so the probability of your observing at t_3 that the constants are right is the same regardless of whether it was God or chance that set the values of the physical constants at t_1. In the firing squad example, if you are alive at t_2, that leaves open what the firing squad decided at t_1 that it will do just after t_2; in consequence, your observing at t_3 that you are alive provides evidence about the squad's decision at t_1 (Sober 2009, p. 86). The fact that you are alive at t_2 induces an OSE in fine-tuning but not in the firing squad example.

Notice that the tables for fine-tuning and the firing squad are the same with respect to their right-hand columns. Maybe this is why the two problems seem similar. However, as mentioned, that similarity is evidentially irrelevant. My exclusive focus on left-hand columns in these three examples reflects an earlier point. Whether you are the victim of an OSE is an objective fact about your actual process of observation; your uncertainty about the character of that process is irrelevant.

5.7 The Multiverse

In discussing the FTA, I have compared God and chance, but there is a third hypothesis to consider. Both the God and chance hypotheses assume that there is a single universe. The multiverse hypothesis asserts that there are infinitely many universes that are causally unconnected with each other. All universes are governed by the same laws, but the values of the constants in those laws can differ across universes, owing to the fact that values in universes are set independently by a single mindless chance process.[76] The multiverse hypothesis make it overwhelmingly probable that some universe or other will have constants that are life-permitting, so we have the following equality:

---

[76] This raises the mathematical problem that was discussed in §5.1.

Table 3 (Fishing)
Pr(you observe at t_3 that the net contains fish all more than 10 in. long | —)

		Possible Processes	
		You put a net with big holes in the lake at t_2.	You put a net with small holes in the lake at t_2.
Hypotheses	100% of the fish in the lake are more than 10 inches long at t_1.	(‖)	(=) (V)
	50% of the fish in the lake are more than 10 inches long at t_1.		(>)

Table 4 (Fine-Tuning)
Pr(you observe at t_3 that the constants are right | —)

		Possible Processes	
		You are alive at t_2.	You are not alive at t_2.
Hypotheses	God sets the constants at t_1.	(>)	0
		(‖)	(‖)
	Chance sets the constants at t_1.	(>)	0

Table 5 (Firing Squad)
Pr(you observe at t_3 that you are alive | —)

		Possible Processes	
		You are alive at t_2.	You are not alive at t_2.
Hypotheses	Squad decides at t_1 that they will spare you when they fire just after t_2.	(>)	0
		(V)	(‖)
	Squad decides at t_1 that they will kill you when they fire just after t_2.	(>)	0

Pr(some universe has constants that are life-permitting | Multiverse) =
Pr(some universe has constants that are life-permitting | God fixed the values of the constants in our Universe),

which entails that the observation cited fails to favor God over the multiverse. This equality is true, but so is the following inequality:

Pr(our universe has constants that are life-permitting | Multiverse) <
Pr(our universe has constants that are life-permitting | God chose the constants in our Universe).

The principle of total evidence (§2.9) entails that you should use "*our* universe has constants that are life-permitting" rather than "*some* universe has constants that are life-permitting" (Hacking 1987; White 2000; Sober 2003). In addition, there is an OSE here, and recognizing it leads you to replace this last inequality with a likelihood equality, though it is not the one displayed in the present paragraph. I invite you to formulate that equality.

Roger White (2015) discusses the multiverse hypothesis in the context of representing the FTA as an inference to the best explanation.[77] He says that the FTA assumes that it needs to be explained why life is possible in our universe. This premise is wrong, White argues, if the multiverse hypothesis is true, since that hypothesis removes the need to explain why life is possible in our universe; the hypothesis has that effect, White says, because it entails that the existence of life in some universe or other is overwhelmingly probable. White defends this assessment by proposing an analogy: when Jack wins a lottery, there is no need to explain why he, rather than Jill, was the winner, if the lottery is fair and each bought a single ticket. After all, it was a certainty that *someone* would win. Notice how White's treatment of the FTA as an inference to the best explanation differs from my likelihood formulation, which says nothing about what *needs to be explained*. The question I considered is whether a given observation is *evidence* that discriminates between hypotheses.

I agree with White that the multiverse hypothesis, if true, removes the need to explain why the constants are right in our universe rather than in some other universe. This is because I still endorse a principle I described in Sober (1986):

H explains why E_1 rather than E_2 is true only if $\Pr(E_1 \mid H) > \Pr(E_2 \mid H)$.

It follows that the multiverse hypothesis cannot explain why there is life in our universe rather than in another. The reason *we* don't need to explain this fact, if the multiverse hypothesis is true, is supplied by the ought-implies-can

---

[77] Recall the claim in §3.6 that likelihood arguments and inferences to the best explanation are different.

principle. However, it does not follow that the existence of life in our universe, rather than in some other, requires no explanation; what follows is just a conditional – no explanation is needed (or possible) *if* the multiverse hypothesis is true.[78]

5.8 Concluding Comments

I argued in this section that the FTA faces a mathematical problem that can be solved, but that two other problems cut deeper. The first focuses on the FTA's assumption that God is life-loving. I see no way to provide that assumption with an independent justification. The second problem is that the FTA is vitiated by an observation selection effect (an OSE).

OSEs undermine cosmic design arguments besides the FTA. For example:

- The observation that the universe contains conscious beings doesn't favor God over chance if this observation is made by observers who are themselves conscious.
- The observation that the universe contains matter does not favor God over chance if this observation is made by observers who have bodies.
- The observation that the universe is orderly doesn't favor God over chance if the existence of the observers making this observation requires there to be order.

How might the grip of an OSE be broken? A good start would be to enrich the observations – to move from logically weaker to logically stronger formulations of what you observe. For example, instead of saying merely that matter exists, you might add details (e.g., about the distribution of matter in the universe). However, that way forward permits another problem to arise – the problem of discerning God's goals with enough clarity that you can tell whether God or chance renders the enriched observation more probable. The FTA and its ilk seem to be caught between a rock and a hard place.

---

[78] Notice also that the reason the multiverse hypothesis can't explain why this universe rather than that one is life-permitting is *not* that the hypothesis says that the existence of a life-permitting universe is overwhelmingly probable.

References

Aquinas, T. (1981). *The Summa Theologica of Saint Thomas Aquinas.* Christian Classics.

Arbuthnot, J. (1710). "An Argument for Divine Providence, Taken from the Constant Regularity Observ'd in the Births of Both Sexes." *Philosophical Transactions of the Royal Society* 27: 186–190.

Bartha, P. (2016). "Analogy and Analogical Reasoning." The Stanford Encyclopedia of Philosophy, E. Zalta (ed.), https://plato.stanford.edu /archives/win2016/entries/reasoning-analogy/.

Behe, M. (1996). *Darwin's Black Box: The Biochemical Challenge to Evolution.* Free Press.

(2004). "Irreducible Complexity: Obstacle to Darwinian Evolution." In W. Dembski and M. Ruse (eds.), *Debating Design: From Darwin to DNA.* Cambridge University Press, pp. 352–370.

(2006). "Whether Intelligent Design Is Science: A Response to the Opinion of the Court in Kitzmiller vs Dover Area School District." Discovery Institute Web Site. www.discovery.org/f/697.

Branch, G. (2017). "Paley the Plagiarist?" https://ncse.com/blog/2017/01/ paley-plagiarist-0018388.

Buckland, W. (1836). *Geology and Mineralogy Considered with Reference to Natural Theology Vol. 1.* The Perfect Library, 2015.

Cairn-Smith, A. G. (1982). *Genetic Takeover and the Mineral Origins of Life.* Cambridge University Press.

Carter, B. (1974). "Large Number Coincidences and the Anthropic Principle in Cosmology." In M. Longair (ed.), *Confrontation of Cosmological Theories with Observational Data.* Reidel, pp. 291–298.

Clutton-Brock, T. and Harvey, P. (1977). "Primate Ecology and Social Organization." *Journal of the Zoological Society of London* 183: 1–39.

Collins, R. (2003). "Evidence for Fine-Tuning." In N. Manson (ed.), *God and Design.* Routledge, pp. 178–199.

(2009). "The Teleological Argument: An Exploration of the Fine-Tuning of the Universe." In W. Craig and J. Moreland (eds.), *The Blackwell Companion to Natural Theology.* Wiley-Blackwell, pp. 202–281.

Colyvan, M., Garfield, J., and Priest, G. (2005). "Problems with the Argument from Fine Tuning." *Synthese* 145: 325–338.

Crow, J. (1979). "Genes That Violate Mendel's Rules." *Scientific American* 240: 134–146.

Darwin, C. (1859). *On the Origin of Species.* Harvard University Press, 1964.

(1871). *The Descent of Man and Selection in Relation to Sex.* Murray.

(1874). *The Descent of Man and Selection in Relation to Sex.* Murray, 2nd edition.

Dawkins, R. (1976). *The Selfish Gene.* Oxford University Press.

(1986). *The Blind Watchmaker.* Norton.

Dembski, W. (1998a). *The Design Inference.* Cambridge University Press.

(1998b). "Intelligent Science and Design." *First Things* 86: 21–27.

Doolittle, W. F. and Sapienza, C. (1980). "Selfish Genes, the Phenotype Paradigm and Genome Evolution." Nature 284: 601–603.

Draper, P. (1989). "Pain and Pleasure: An Evidential Problem for Theists." *Noûs* 23: 331–350.

Duhem, P. (1914). *The Aim and Structure of Physical Theory.* Princeton University Press, 1954.

Earman, J. (1987). "The SAP Also Rises: A Critical Examination of the Anthropic Principle." *American Philosophical Quarterly* 24: 307–317.

Eddington, A. (1939). *The Philosophy of Physical Science.* Cambridge University Press.

Edwards, A. (1972). *Likelihood.* Cambridge University Press.

Everitt, N. (2003). The Non-Existence of God. Routledge.

Fisher, R. (1930). *The Genetical Theory of Natural Selection.* Oxford University Press.

(1956). *Statistical Methods and Scientific Inference.* Oliver and Boyd.

Fitelson, B. (2011). "Favoring, Likelihoods, and Bayesianism." *Philosophy and Phenomenological Research* 8: 666–672.

Fitelson, B., Stephens, C., and Sober, E. (1999). "How Not to Detect Design, a Review of William Dembski's *The Design Inference.*" *Philosophy of Science* 66: 472–488.

Forrest, B. and Gross, P. (2004). *Creationism's Trojan Horse: The Wedge of Intelligent Design.* Oxford University Press.

Forster, M. (2006). "Counterexamples to a Likelihood Theory of Evidence." *Minds and Machines* 16: 319–338.

Forster, M. and Sober, E. (2004). "Why Likelihood?" In M. Taper and S. Lee (eds.), *The Nature of Scientific Evidence.* University of Chicago Press, pp. 153–165.

Gould, S. (1980). "The Panda's Thumb." In *The Panda's Thumb*, Norton, pp. 19–26.

Hacking, I. (1965). *The Logic of Statistical Inference.* Cambridge University Press.

(1987). "The Inverse Gambler's Fallacy: The Argument from Design and the Anthropic Principle Applied to Wheeler Universes." *Mind* 96: 331–340.

Horwich, P. (1982). *Probability and Evidence*. Cambridge University Press.

Howson, C. and Urbach, P. (1993). *Scientific Reasoning: The Bayesian Approach*. Open Court.

Hume, D. (1779). *Dialogues Concerning Natural Religion*. D. Coleman (ed.), Cambridge University Press, 2007.

Jantzen, B. (2014). *An Introduction to Design Arguments*. Cambridge University Press.

Jeffrey, R. (1965). *The Logic of Decision*. University of Chicago Press, 2nd edition, 1983.

Johnson, P. (1991). *Darwin on Trial*. InterVarsity Press, 2nd edition, 1993.

Kingsolver, J. and Koehl, M. (1985). "Aerodynamics, Thermoregulation, and the Evolution of Insect Wings: Differential Scaling and Evolutionary Change." *Evolution* 39: 488–504.

Kitcher, P. (1983). *Abusing Science*. MIT Press.

Kolmogorov, A. N. (1950). *Foundations of the Theory of Probability*. Chelsea.

Kotzen, M. (2012). "Selection Biases in Likelihood Arguments." *British Journal for the Philosophy of Science* 63: 825–839.

Krebs, J. and Davies, N. (1981). *An Introduction to Behavioral Ecology*. Sinauer.

Le Poidevin, R. (1996). *Arguing for Atheism*. Routledge.

Leslie, J. (1989). *Universes*. Routledge.

Lipton, P. (2004). *Inference to the Best Explanation*. Routledge, 2nd edition.

Lloyd, E. (2017). "Units and Levels of Selection." The Stanford Encyclopedia of Philosophy, E. Zalta (ed.), https://plato.stanford.edu/archives/sum2017/entries/selection-units/.

McGrew, L. (2004). "Testability, Likelihoods, and Design." *Philo* 7: 5–21.

(2016). "Four (or so) New Fine-Tuning Arguments." *European Journal for Philosophy of Religion* 8: 85–106.

McGrew, T., McGrew, L., and Vestrup, E. (2001). "Probabilities and the Fine-Tuning Argument: A Sceptical View." *Mind* 110: 1027–1037.

Meyer, S. (2009). *Signature in the Cell: DNA and the Evidence for Intelligent Design*. Harper Collins.

Monton, B. (2006). "God, Fine-Tuning, and the Problem of Old Evidence." *British Journal for the Philosophy of Science* 57: 405–424.

Morris, H. (1980). *King of Creation*. CLP Publishers.

Narveson, J. (2003). "God by Design?" in N. Manson (ed.), *God and Design*. Routledge, pp. 88–104.

Numbers, R. (2004). "Ironic Heresy: How Young-Earth Creationists Came to Embrace Rapid Microevolution by Means of Natural Selection." In A. Lustig, R. Richards, and M. Ruse (eds.), *Darwinian Heresies*. Cambridge University Press, pp. 84–104.

O'Connor, D. (2001). Hume on Religion. Routledge.

Oppy, G. (2002). "Paley's Argument for Design." *Philo* 5.2: 161–173.

Orgel, L. & Crick, F. (1980). "Selfish DNA: The Ultimate Parasite." *Nature* 284: 604–607.

Orr, H. A. (1997). "Darwin v. Intelligent Design (Again)." Boston Review, December/January. pp. 41–54.

Orzack, S. and Sober, E. (1994). "Optimality Models and the Test of Adaptationism." *American Naturalist* 143: 361–380.

Paley, W. (1802). *Natural Theology, or, Evidences of the Existence and Attributes of the Deity, Collected from the Appearances of Nature.* Rivington.

Palazzo, A. and Gregory, T. (2014). "The Case for Junk DNA." *PLOS Genetics* 10.5: e1004351. https://doi.org/10.1371/journal.pgen.1004351

Priest, G. (1981). "The Argument from Design." *Australasian Journal of Philosophy* 59: 422–431.

Psillos, S. (2007). "The Fine Structure of Inference to the Best Explanation." *Philosophy and Phenomenological Research* 74: 441–448.

Pyle, A. (2006). *Hume's Dialogues Concerning Natural Religion: A Reader's Guide.* Bloomsbury.

Roberts, J. (2012). "Fine-Tuning and the Infrared Bulls-Eye." *Philosophical Studies* 160: 287–303.

Robson, J. (1990). "The Fiat and Finger of God: The Bridgewater Treatises". In R. Helmstadter, B. ; Lightman, and V. Bernard (eds.). *Victorian Faith in Crisis: Essays on Continuity and Change in Nineteenth-Century Religious Belief.* Stanford University Press

Royall, R. (1997). *Statistical Evidence: A Likelihood Paradigm.* Chapman & Hall/CRC.

Russell, R. (1912). "On the Notion of Cause." *Proceedings of the Aristotelian Society* 13: 1–26.

Salmon, W. (1978). "Religion and Science: A New Look at Hume's Dialogues." *Philosophical Studies* 33: 143–176.

Sarkar, S. (2007). *Doubting Darwin: Creationist Designs of Evolution.* Blackwell.

Schupbach, J. (2005). "Paley's Inductive Inference to Design." *Philosophia Christi* 7: 2.

Sedley, D. (2007). *Creationism and Its Critics in Antiquity.* University of California Press.

Shanks, N. and Joplin, K. (1999). "Redundant Complexity: A Critical Analysis of Intelligent Design in Biochemistry." *Philosophy of Science* 66: 268–282.

Shimony, A. (1970). "Scientific Inference." In R. Colodny (ed.), *The Nature and Function of Scientific Theories.* University of Pittsburgh Press.

Shapiro, A. (2009). "William Paley's 'Lost' Intelligent Design." *History and Philosophy of the Life Sciences* 31: 55–77.

Sober, E. (1984). *The Nature of Selection.* MIT Press.

(1986). "Explanatory Presupposition." *Australasian Journal of Philosophy* 64: 143–149.

(1990). *Core Questions in Philosophy: A Text with Readings.* Macmillan.

(1993). *Philosophy of Biology.* Westview Press.

(1999). "Testability." *Proceedings and Addresses of the American Philosophical Association* 73: 47–76.

(2002). "Intelligent Design and Probability Reasoning." *International Journal for the Philosophy of Religion* 52: 65–80.

(2003). "The Argument from Design." In N. Manson (ed.), *God and Design.* Routledge, pp. 25–53. Reprinted in W. Mann (ed.), *The Blackwell Guide to Philosophy of Religion,* 2004, pp. 117–147.

(2004). "Likelihood, Model Selection, and the Duhem-Quine Problem." *Journal of Philosophy* 101: 1–22.

(2007a). "Intelligent Design Theory and the Supernatural: The 'God or Extra-Terrestrials' Reply." *Faith and Philosophy* 24: 72–82.

(2007b). "What's Wrong with Intelligent Design?" *Quarterly Review of Biology* 82: 1–8.

(2008). *Evidence and Evolution: The Logic Behind the Science.* Cambridge University Press.

(2009). "Absence of Evidence and Evidence of Absence: Evidential Transitivity in Connection with Fossils, Fishing, Fine-Tuning, and Firing Squads." *Philosophical Studies* 143: 63–90.

(2011). *Did Darwin Write the* Origin *Backwards?* Prometheus Books.

(2012). "Coincidences and How to Think about Them." In *European Philosophy of Science Association Proceedings 2009,* Springer, pp. 355–374.

(2015). *Ockham's Razors: A User's Manual.* Cambridge University Press.

(forthcoming-a). "A Bayesian Double Negative: A Critique of Hume's Treatment of the Design Argument in the *Dialogues* and of the Design

Argument Itself." In K. Williford (ed.), *Essays on Hume's Dialogues Concerning Natural Religion*. Routledge.

(forthcoming-b). "Is Fine-Tuning Evidence for God's Existence? No." In M. Peterson and R. VanArragon (eds.), *Contemporary Debates in Philosophy of Religion*. Wiley-Blackwell, 2nd edition.

Sober, E. and Orzack, J. (2003). "Common Ancestry and Natural Selection." *British Journal for the Philosophy of Science* 54: 423–437.

Sober, E. and Steel, M. (2002). "Testing the Hypothesis of Common Ancestry." *Journal of Theoretical Biology* 218: 395–408.

(2017). "Similarities as Evidence for Common Ancestry: A Likelihood Epistemology." *British Journal for the Philosophy of Science* 68: 617–638.

Sober, E. & Wilson, D. (1998). *Unto Others*. Harvard University Press.

Swinburne, R. (1968). "The Argument from Design." *Philosophy* 43: 199–212.

(1997). *Simplicity As Evidence of Truth*. Marquette University Press.

(2004). *The Existence of God*. Oxford University Press. 2nd edition, 2010.

Titelbaum, M. (2013). *Quitting Certainties: A Bayesian Framework Modeling Degrees of Belief*. New York, NY: Oxford University Press.

Tversky, A. & Kahneman, D. (1982a). "Evidential Impact of Base Rates." In D. Kahneman, P. Slovic, & A. Tversky (eds.), *Judgment Under Uncertainty: Heuristics and Biases*. Cambridge University Press, pp. 153–160.

(1982b). "Judgments of and by Representativeness." In D. Kahneman, P. Slovic, & A. Tversky (eds.), *Judgment Under Uncertainty: Heuristics and Biases*. Cambridge University Press, pp. 84–98.

van Fraassen, B. (1989). *Laws and Symmetry*. Clarendon Press.

Vassend, O, Sober, E., and Fitelson, B. (2017). "The Philosophical Significance of Stein's Paradox." *European Journal for the Philosophy of Science* 7: 411–433.

Venn, J. (1866). *The Logic of Chance*. Chelsea Publishing.

Weisberg, J. (2005). "Firing Squads and Fine-Tuning: Sober on the Design Argument." *British Society for the Philosophy of Science* 56: 809–821.

(2010). "A Note on Design: What's Fine-Tuning Got to Do with It?" *Analysis* 70.3: 431–438.

Wells, J. (2011). *The Myth of Junk DNA*. Discovery Institute Press.

Whewell, W. (1833). *Astronomy and General Physics Considered with Reference to Natural Theology*. Kessinger Publishing, 2014.

White, R. (2000). "Fine-Tuning and Multiple Universes." *Nous* 34: 260–276.

(2015). "The Argument from Cosmological Fine-Tuning." In G. Rosen, A. Byrne, J. Cohen, and S. Shiffrin (eds.), *The Norton Introduction to Philosophy*. Norton, pp. 45–50.

Zach, R. (1978). "Selection and Dropping of Whelks by Northwestern Crows." *Behaviour* 67: 134–148.

Zhang, J. and Zhang, K. (2015). "Likelihood and Consilience: On Forster's Counterexamples to the Likelihood Theory of Evidence." *Philosophy of Science* 82: 930–940.

for Ruby Louise Sober

Acknowledgments

I thank Joel Ballivian, Emily Barrett, Elizabeth Bell, Dylan Beschoner, Glenn Branch, Jeremy Butterfield, Mike Byrd, Frank Cabrera, Patrick Cronin, Katherine Deaven, Ford Doolittle, Jordan Ellenberg, Camila Hernandez Flowerman, Andrea Guardo, Stephanie Hoffmann, Paul Kelly, Lydia McGrew, Sean Leibowitz, Thomas Liu, Steven Nadler, Shannon Nolen, Ronald Numbers, Steve Orzack, Jim Paulson, Katie Petrik, William Roche, Michael Ruse, Larry Shapiro, Lindley Slipetz, Mike Steel, Reuben Stern, Michael Titelbaum, Jonathon Vandenhombergh, Olav Vassend, Peter Vranas, Kenneth Williford, and Aaron Yarmel for useful discussion, and Yujin Nagasawa, editor of this series, for his assistance.

I owe a special thanks to Benjamin C. Jantzen for the extensive, helpful comments he provided when he refereed my manuscript for Cambridge University Press. I'm also grateful to the William F. Vilas Trust of the University of Wisconsin for financial support.

Some of Section 2 comes from Sober (2015) and some of Section 5 comes from Sober (forthcoming-b). My thanks to the publishers for permitting me to use this material.

Cambridge Elements

Philosophy of Religion

Yujin Nagasawa
University of Birmingham
Yujin Nagasawa is Professor of Philosophy and Co-Director of the John Hick Centre for
Philosophy of Religion at the University of Birmingham. He is currently President of the
British Society for the Philosophy of Religion. He is a member of the Editorial Board of
Religious Studies, the *International Journal for Philosophy of Religion* and *Philosophy
Compass*.

About the Series
This Cambridge Elements series provides concise and structured introductions to all the
central topics in the philosophy of religion. It offers balanced, comprehensive coverage of
multiple perspectives in the philosophy of religion. Contributors to the series are cutting-
edge researchers who approach central issues in the philosophy of religion. Each provides
a reliable resource for academic readers and develops new ideas and arguments from a
unique viewpoint.

Cambridge Elements ☰

Philosophy of Religion

Made in the USA
Monee, IL
20 December 2020

54358742R00056